AN ANTHOLOGY OF LOVE

Sree

INDIA • SINGAPORE • MALAYSIA

ISBN
Hardcase 979-8-89588-359-4
Paperback 979-8-89556-011-2

for Her
-who, i adore….

Contents

Preface

The boundaries of being sane, runs thin, when it is about someone you love. I am proud to be reasonably insane – to love this girl, beyond human means.

A few years ago, I wouldn't have known what it would have meant to be the person I am today. In not just saying this aloud but living this life every day – I play roles I never thought I could, lest imagine what they meant. Through her means of loving me back, she taught me love, beyond what is seen or heard, spoken or read, dreamt or lived!

She is the artist of connecting dots and remembering the things that harm me, in ways unfathomable to the male brain. Thus, what may seem far from figuring out - for the rest of the world - she ensures, will be done at ease. My girl! In saying that with utmost caution - she is an explosive charge ready to unleash her wrath, if disrespected!

She carries herself on a pedestal - too high to reach. One may ask for a reason behind my mortal means to win her love. There was a time when she loved me – during the times of yore! Having lived through those lovely days, I can only hope that my tomorrow will inch towards, what seemed like a dream!

I do not see my love as a red-flag, neither to me, nor to my girl – as the slightest clue of inconvenience on her face, freezes me cold! From the moment I open my eyes, till I hear her "Good night", I relish the confectionary of her melody and love – I cannot explain how! My desire to see her, talk to her, hold her, touch her, whisper sweet nothings into her ears is the hope that builds me in the morning and burns me at night!

I stand to share with you my choicest collection of poems, written, thinking of her, while penning down each alphabet. I drown to the abyss, when I miss her – even when she sits right across. Although she does not get my physiological condition in her absence, she tries her best to not to make me crave for her – this I am aware!

In a world as dark as this, she is the beam of light; while in a night so dark as a mess, she is the beacon of my life! One who may read these poems may connect better, knowing that – She is the one who never says yes, and he is the one who never says No!

Sree-

Girl Love

There were times when I missed her bad. As she spoke with bright, eager eyes about something that had excited her that day, I found myself mesmerized and momentarily lost. I'd gaze into those deep, expressive eyes and marvel at how nature had crafted such a remarkable person and bestowed her upon me. In every facet of who she is, and in everything she has woven into our lives, she is a boundless reservoir of beauty and love.

What is to nature,
When all is but creature,
Life barely exists,
Love, the only feature!

A child to a mother,
Hanging by a tether,
Between all the cries,
Only happy together!

In the lap of mountains,
Below the tree curtains,
Grows a lake pristine,
Beauty there pertains!

Of such is a girl,
A one of a pearl,
What makes her so,
Shades in a whirl!

Maybe so people call,
To either, a man may fall,
To the one and only flavor,
Wondering, life can stall!

True love is far,
The path can scar,
Destiny is all worth,
There, you are a star!

Shimmer of morn sun,
A dew glitter can stun,
Such will feel the heart,
To your girl, a run!

A look from far above,
Life seems - just now,
Though a far beginning,
There is nothing but love!

Her in my Mind

Obsession is often a misunderstood human concept, coined to describe the overwhelming fixation on someone or something. If you've ever experienced waking up consumed by thoughts of someone, drifting through your daily routines while dreaming about how to spend time with them, then you understand my predicament here. I grapple with a need to remind myself, to step back from this consuming passion—she only agrees.

Some days are very rough,
As if time should pass, enough,
I wonder why only me,
And nobody else seems to see!

On a few, it starts so dull,
Hours, the mood on a mull,
The mind starts to cut-chew,
Crazy though, thoughts in all hue!

There is only her, I trouble,
I pull her into my plastic bubble,
While being all sad and caustic,
I drive her to actions, drastic!

She tries to put in some sense,
To me, it seems sharp and tense,
Being clingy, it is all painful,
Her words are all right and truthful!

I am better, past year to three,
Admire her patience and just agree,
She is the only light I seek,
In the dark days that make me meek!

When I am sick, she is my pills,
My dry heart pot, in love she fills,
The dry senseless world around,
Fades away in her aura abound!

In a man there is just flaw,
Like an animal he can only thaw,
This is the fear I live in today,
In another man, if she may lay!

In all the drama and tantrum,
I put her on spot in a cauldron,
Like an angel she sweeps my mind,
Lifts me from ashes, she's a Phoenix, kind!

Woman, they say is the source,
In my life, she decides the course,
How I see her affection grow,
In front of me, she melts in slow!

You Love me!

At times, my girl displays a charming modesty, a recent development where she hints at things, leaving me to guess. Though I often succeed, but at times her intricate mind keeps me endlessly intrigued and exploring. She can only say that she loves me, but we both know - she can't step in further. When I ask her this, she doesn't disagree!

How do I start to speak of you,
So vast and abundant in view,
Maybe about what you mean,
To me and to the world be seen!

Guess no one can get it right,
How I hold you in my heart, tight,
How they judge through prying eyes,
I only see their thoughts, vice!

Like you say, I maybe wrong,
In singing to you all night long,
Things could've been a lot different,
If not for little souvenirs and scent!

When in times we run out of clue,
Yes, we'd hold each other like glue,
Why is it so, any fool may ask,
As between us, we have no mask!

Unlike you think, maybe it is love,
A little just over a friend and above,
The walls are barely there you see,
Without which, happy we can be!

There is a big reason, we both know,
It was always there, even when low,
When it never for once stood so tall,
Why should it now, just break the wall!

Come closer, lets rewrite the stars,
Misaligned by a decade of wars,
We know how good we are together,
We fly in life's winds like a feather!

If picture perfect had a model,
Many of us outside in cuddle,
How much longer should I wait to hear,
Should I walk in miles to get you near!

Burns to hear about the ideal man,
What am I short of, in the clan,
You say there is none close by,
Nobody by my pedestal so high!

Oh Fuhrer! My Fuhrer!

When I use this term, I speak only of my supreme leader. She governs every aspect of my life—my frowns, my smiles, my steps, and my tears. To call me a puppet would be an understatement, for a puppet lacks even a semblance of autonomy. I possess a will and desire, yet entirely at her command, swaying only to her slightest nod.

I learnt about dating,
Be together without stating,
Guess it works for a few,
May not, for my girl - a dew!

She is eager to go and try,
About it, my hearts a fry,
Tells me I am a friend - so true,
My day is now, but a screw!

Not that she doesn't know,
Me madly in love, asks so?
She is proud to call me an ex,
I know now, I'm her annex!

Don't dare judge my princess,
Of Royalty, she is no less,

In all the bad things she does,
I am the only one for her fuss!

In all of this, I take pride,
Her face is my life's slide,
Out of pains and struggle always,
Here thus, I rest my case!

Says, with me she's frank,
Talks, its mostly a prank,
Why baby, you take it light,
I know, for me - the world you'll fight!

All the songs are futile,
Waiting, a day is - a while,
Smiling beauty to me, walking,
A guilty smile, a minute of talking!

My touch ends up a gasp,
Close to you, in a love clasp,
I know the next day is terror,
Here I say, Aye Aye Fuhrer!

Epiphany

I come from humble beginnings, characterized by modesty, politeness, and a light spirit. To live without deeper meaning is to live like an animal. As humans, we grapple - not with primal fears, but with the anxiety of loss and distress—the fear of rejection or abandonment. An emotion I wrestle with daily: the thought of what if she chooses someone else, even if she might never not.

Common is a mental seizure,
When there's none to love and nurture,
The lovely one, who is now so close,
May walk away to the life they chose!

You may sit on a bald rock,
What went wrong, taking stock,
Is this all there is to living,
Wondering what is it about giving?

All that you poured on them,
Nursed the wounds and help stem,
Falling in love counting to ten,
They became your life, after then!

You can't unlove, maybe a curse,
In that fear, chant many a verse,
The one you love may find some other,
You still hung tight on their tether!

The thought of them with another,
Burns deep in through your leather,
How you can't anymore stand,
Thinking, on them - someone's hand!

How the other may make them feel,
Blinded love, you wish them happy be,
Advice your person what not to do,
Never step down for that one, even if due!

In all this pain, you forget your age,
At a point, where you can be a sage,
By not letting them go, you are in trouble,
Doing so, you will end up in a rubble!

All life's guide is from only wise,
Who haven't known what is so nice,
In the memory, you dread to relive,
The Harsh reality is so hard to believe!

I

In all the poems I've written, I've seldom spoken of myself. This one is different; it reflects who I am. It captures a time when my pain was profound in her absence, and my longing for her love drove me to put pen to paper.

I have a bad urge today,
A lot of things I want to say,
Quite sure it will be painful,
I want to stop feeling dreadful!

I have drowned a many time,
Always scared of water and pines,
Yet I end up in both or either,
Or sulking, as I sit by there!

What if I pray to God once,
To make me deaf and mute thence,
I will live along with no senses,
The world will not have grievances!

I held it up against people,
Who, bad to me with a label,
For once I felt benevolent,
Forgave them all without a vent!

Thought this would ease my life,
Or so the shrink says, give up strife,
After all of this an endeavor,
My mornings are still dull and sour!

Now I do have only a few,
To run to and show them my hue,
They are all mostly patient,
With my outbursts, often pungent!

How should I be?

Each day, I reshape myself, contemplating how she would like me to look, speak, and act. I ponder how she might envision herself beside me and how I should gracefully align with her wishes. Despite having the power to cast me aside or drive me to madness, she remains my lioness, capable of guiding me with a mere touch. As I write this poem, I come to recognize her influence and reflect on my own futile efforts to seek her presence.

If on some day, I ever can,
Walk to the past, against the ban,
Talk to myself, foolishly so,
Tell what is here, ask not to go!

How the learned always say,
Time is relative, never at bay,
I only know now, what they mean,
Imagining things I have once seen!

The mind is stuck in a tesseract,
All means to escape are false and fact,
Thoughts can beam across universe,
With time passing in seconds, a curse!

It builds a world of itself fast,
Stitching future and memories from past,
Before you know, you are hallucinating,
Is it in real or fake, you keep stating!

You're never sad when asleep,
Is that the way, I should seek,
A small kid says, you keep busy,
To live serene and avoid being fuzzy!

I feel very sorry for being myself,
Appear to beg and grovel, to shelf,
My feelings so many, already packed,
Maybe I want myself to be stacked!

Not that, to people I never tell,
What is in my mind, I often yell,
Knowing it all, the ones I call mine,
Fire at me back, saying I whine!

Now I stand unclothed defense-less,
When you stab me, not making a mess,
I hold my pieces, that you chopped wary,
My blood stained your clothes, I am sorry!

Even through this pain gut-wrench,
Stand tall, in my hope I drench,
Maybe it was just a bad phase,
Or so my horoscope says, take a pace!

Superstition is for the weak,
I don't disagree, I am a meek,
In saying all this, I hope today,
Will be, I need not say May-Day!

Might of a Girl

The wise say - a girl holds the power and key, to all happiness and despair of the world. For I do not challenge the wise, I can only agree. In all of herself, she is mystical and strong, deceitful and wrong! To win over such a lover is hard – and as of my girl, even dreaming is retard!

To love a woman is hard,
Ready to be called retard,
More so if with a broken heart,
Patiently pick up each shard!

In her twenties she is sweet,
A girl who never calls retreat,
Holds her swords and calls Charge,
A moment later she'll smile and greet!

If she has found her mate,
She will, for them, renounce her fate,
In giving all of herself in,
Sometimes self she'll hate!

By her thirties, she's taken hits,
From everybody, in mighty bits,
She's often paved way to life,
Her hands are burnt even with mitts!

She's by now, a royal savage,
Treat her unwell, she'll be no sage,
Her wisdom is now a mighty tree,
By now she knows how to gage!

Charge at her, and you will know,
A tigress with cubs, crouching low,
The only way to her is by love,
If you mess up, a mighty blow!

Come to forties, she's an angel,
Ignore your squabble and no cajole,
The sweet girl is now deep inside,
Her outer sheath, nothing fragile!

In all through this, she's a girl,
Is one of natures' best living pearl,
All she wants is to be nurtured,
In asking for this, she will hurl!

Her Highness

She is my queen, my princess and all of royalty – and she commands that position in my heart. Although benevolent and kind, a wrong move will end me up in punishment unkind. While the gory part of life remains, her lap and lips make me give her my reins.

There is beauty in many a form,
Women, they are one of the norm,
While, there is not much to wonder,
How a man's mind starts to ponder!
    They all are a beauty - no doubt,
    More so when they flaunt their pout,
    In seeing all these happen, I think,
    Why the only one, I see with no blink!
She is unique in more than one ways,
Smile, can slow down my hearts pace,
In wit, she is a queen unparalleled,
In love, I feel my knees are now felled!
    What is it that makes me love her so,
    Rough, Rude, she shouts at me to go,
    Uncut, she is my sole found diamond,
    To hold her I become the tree, stunned!

Today I found out what was true,
She's a woman who talks not to woo,
In my arms, she is the all powerful,
Staying so, she loves me back plentiful!

Things she makes me do!

Going all the way, is a futile effort of someone telling all that they do for another. If you love someone, as much, all the way - will never exist, as that will be the only way. Such is my lover, where she is my journey, and my destiny.

To love a girl is divine,
Drenched in her thought,
In counting one to nine,
At ten, she's the only sought!

To wake up every morn,
Dreaming of just a day,
While her picture I adorn,
Wondering what she may say!

To meet her later is a wish,
Wondering what she may wear,
Her boundless beauty is a bliss,
Her absence I cannot bear!

To love her more than life,
Something I never could guess,
Could she be my wife,
That would be so much less!

To wait for her again,
Is a sweet pain so dear,
She is now a stubborn stain,
All my heart, I smear!

To think what is that in her,
That makes me fly above,
Drops of love, like honey were,
She had rained on me, how!

To be loved by her, a boon,
How I pray for those days back,
Walk along under the moon,
Close to her without slack!

Absolute is Nothing

In loving my girl, I collected no souvenirs. Not her picture, nor her things, nothing about - when we had wings! Only memories in our minds that are deep into us – and the tiny ones that surface – once, when blue moon does!

We are often lost ourselves,
Relics - we stack in shelves,
Not knowing what is next,
Without a clue of pretext!

There may be miracles a few,
Angels may descend too,
It is in, how these things play,
One often feels, made of clay!

Everyone is the same around,
Maybe there are a few found,
They can steer your ship to,
Inspire you about things to do!

Some say these ones are sent,
We tag them and name ignorant,
It is in just how one sees,
Is it the honey, or the bees?

Some always win in solitude,
Some others in methods - crude,
We don't have to win the world,
Or so are the losers told!

What is it you are up to,
Is it God, or your virtue?
None may see in you a hero,
In the end it all sums to Zero!

We all need one

In times when she was afar, and all my attempts to reach her were in vain – I would slowly sink in my emotions. I would wonder about a happier time and slip into fantasies. Often the reality of life would be masked by this parallel universe – making me write words as below!

On the beach so wide,
We are to face the tide,
A grain in the sand yet,
Try to face the might and bet!

On some walks a crab,
Some of us through a shell's nab,
Some near the tide high,
The sun, some of us Hot Dry!

Occasionally, a froth so white,
In short, life is all in spite,
For there is no selfless,
You end up becoming a mess!

As the water flows over,
The beach loses cover,
Each grain is twice tossed,
Life resumes after being paused!

I am

There was once a tense moment, between us – when I voiced that I was a good man, and I deserved better. However stupid it may seem now, my girl, in all her frankness, countered and told me how I was bad. In having a few good traits and bad as everyone else, I tried these lines, in a desperate attempt to feel better.

I am a gem,
Also a hem,
Maybe gum,
Trying my hum!

I am a pain,
A disdain too,
Painfully cry,
Hopelessly try!

I am lovely,
Clingy maybe,
A shipwreck,
And mind stretch!

I am a Maverick,
A sticky slick,
Sometimes amber,
Dead timber too!

I am love,
And of care,
Watch my grasp,
A tight clasp!

I am loved,
By one and many,
But my love is,
Hell as rainy!

I am strange,
A lot good too,
But mostly bad,
Worse in a few!

Complicated - with Her

One of the most attractive features of my girl is the way she knows her things and how she carries herself through the unknown. What may sound admiration; without boundaries, will only be love. If I must be born again to be hers, I will do it a million times!

She knows she's pretty,
Soft, fair and sweet,
A pink rose may seem petty,
She's nature's feat!

She knows how to look,
Ignores all my wish,
Carries me on fishhook,
Cooks me on a dish!

She knows me so well,
I find it hard to guess,
Sarcasm she does sell,
I wonder how this mess?

She knows how to steer,
My life with hers,
Though I am very near,
Closer, I chant a verse!

She knows it all through,
Confident and bold,
Love with all my heart - true,
In all warm and cold!

She knows I'm her man,
Denies all of love,
Someday she'll turn her van,
She'll be all mine from now!

She knows she is the best,
Far across and wide,
Through a hundred a test,
Will swim to her through a tide!

Magically, She!

Someone once said that it's love that shapes who we become. I'm not so sure about that. To me —my girl is so enchanting that, it's my love that feels extraordinary. From her smile to her frown, from her eyes to her smirks, everything about her is perfect. How else could such perfection exist if not through her?

I love a girl,
Tad little younger,
A natural pearl,
In wisdom, a lot elder!

I love her lips,
For they seldom part,
Her words in strips,
Without me they never start!

I love her eyes,
Deep as the abyss,
Her stare is so nice,
Ends my mind in a mess!

I love the talk,
Where I do the most,
Aside her I walk,
In her flirt, I am a toast!

I love the bold,
She's ready to fight,
Alone, what I am told,
I lose all my might!

I love what is of us,
How we are perfect,
Blend in with no fuss,
We are one, just a dialect!

I love how I love her,
Wide eyes and desperate,
If a war together, we were,
She's the trigger, me the turret!

Nature, She and I

Often the world has a haze between love and romance. While the both of us are in for romance, the love that people call divine, is in no dearth between us. In her thought of how she slept to the thought of where she is – in its entirety, the care, affection, desire, love, encompasses life – on the whole!

About dusk when none's around,
By the shore, a rising moon found,
As the waves lash the pile of sand,
In a beach, to a salty breeze I stand!

In the far forests deep and cool,
Watching a stunted oak, by the pool,
How the birds are diving in and out,
Stream of water from the rocky spout!

The creak of the far swaying bamboo,
Nightjar, one here and another there too,
Oh that is a symphony of noisy crickets,
I pull a jar out, a pair of firefly to pocket!

I rest now, to a bark I push my back,
As the winds blow over a rocks crack,
In Her lap I slip my mind to sleep,
A night that is so peaceful, dark and deep!

A Galaxy away!

Love knows no boundaries, and any attempt to confine it will always fall short. Self-respect, privacy—these lines blur when you're in love. The same applies to physical constraints like time, distance, and speed. In fact, if we weren't together on this earth, our love would still transcend all limits, as if expressed in a poem written across the cosmos.

In another world, a little away,
Light years and a different day,
She and I are strewn apart,
A sliver of hope in our tiny heart!

In pursuit of peace, we are here,
Chose to part, but stay near,
While I fell into a well of pain,
She stayed aground, calling it vain!

Miles apart, I long for her love,
If someone could see us from above,
They would know the what and why,
Spread across space and time - we lie!

In another world, I will now dream,
Given means to go back, it may seem,
Insane enough, I will do now wish,
Someday, go back to her with a swish!

With time, I built a mast and sail,
Through the void I flew marking a tail,
A smile so wide, an excited kid,
Told myself, I am not anyone to bid!

Though I came back, rather slow,
Realizing she was my only glow,
To live with her however she said,
A new person, in me - I tread!

A few fights, and harsh words,
Few more tears, flew away like birds,
It once did get really bad,
Goodbye she said, locking me - sad!

For once I thought, I did lose her,
Gone our days, happy - they were,
Only, if she did - let me back in,
In love, she and I would've win!

Yes, you did guess it right,
She and I were back after a fight,
Now when I see, we only got stronger,
And stand by each other to travel farther!

Yet, there is always a growing fear,
If I cause her trouble enough to tear,
The gentle fabric of our special love,
Melt away like ice on a stove!

Faith, I say - I do have it strong,
In her and our time together, this long,
Like how she is everything, to me now,
I am to her, to her tender hands - I glove!

In the end

Reflecting on all the troubles I cause to my girl – for continuing to love her, despite our break-up. It is not as bad as it sounds – she loves me too, in bits and pieces, in her way. So, in a way, my troubles to her are bitter-sour-sweet-disgusting at the same time!

One who lost everything,
Has nothing more to lose,
Suffered the pain a many,
Laughs at its face too,
Cried all night and day,
Sulked through the wounds,
Moaned, sobbed in snare,
World is in all colorful hue!

This one is a danger,
To the society and you,
Though not harmful,
Will deprive all the glue,
That holds humans together,
Stay away from the pool,
Though it looks very calm,
The undercurrent will kill you!

It is not worth it,
To pull the snare apart,
Stories and do fictions,
Give you a different start,
Say you need to help,
The ones in misery and pain,
Not this one at least,
Never the one standing in rain!

I force myself to say,
Time and again, I swear!
Let them have it their way,
Even if nobody cares,
It is you who goes all the way,
To make it special always,
Just hold your horses,
Smile, nod and yes - you should say!

Maybe you just too much,
For everybody around here,
Guess you were born as such,
To love and hold them dear,
You let all of them to touch,
The innermost of what is you,
Sit back and carefully watch,
They tear it all, it is true!

Pouring it all over a poem,
There is not much you'll achieve,
It is you who is not calm,
For not pushing yourself to leave,
Like they all shout and say,
It is you who is clingy and confused,
It is always your special day,
Killed, gracefully misconstrued!!

That girl

A girl is wiser any day – God created them adding extra strains of wisdom in their brains, and that is evident from birth. With age and life, she will only get stronger – please give up, she is way ahead! On the other hand, she knows what she wants and can read your minds at the snap of her fingers. To win the love of such, is ....

If you love a woman in thirties,
Please give up on subtle sorties,
She is now the goddess of wisdom,
May love her, but want you seldom!

Show her what she means to you,
Not expecting anything she'd do,
Her words won't tell anything now,
If you can't read her eyes, how!

Her words are now mostly sounds,
If you hear it, be blessed to be found,
Nobody can love you back better,
Than that woman, without a letter!

She's a relic, although she's cold,
As ice, sharp and glitter of gold,
If you're not married to her yet,
She'll shower you with her best love, I bet!

Introspect

How I wish I grew a brain,
To think, act and not stain,
Appears that I never learn,
What to say when it's not my turn!

The only hope is out there,
Into the bleak day I stare,
Maybe the next minute is better,
And there maybe a love letter!

I'm so stupid, I do agree,
Maybe some day I will be free,
I wish I could fast forward,
And be much less of this coward!

Yield to her!

In a war, one may surrender, likely so - in sins, some may confess. Sometimes concede, at times give in. But when it is a girl, there is nothing to say – and all is known!

When your girl is very beautiful,
And her love is vast, plentiful,
What can you ask for, oh miser man,
In her glow, you will sure tan!
When her eyes are deep as abyss,
Her lips worthy of such a kiss,
Go on and pray to hold her hand,
If she doesn't veil and wave her wand!
Sit by her, across a small table,
It is true, about her is all the fable,
Lost in thought' what is that so sweet,
Is it the sugar or thought of her feet!
When she will run her fingers by the cheek,
You will know why you are still a meek,
Yield! Give up all your ego mortal soul,
It is now time to end the night in a growl!

Feline Love

Some like dogs, some like birds, some like butterflies, while some like fish. But there are a few who love cats – and they strike differently. Their love is implicit and only feline seems to get it. Such is my girl who is harmed by a cat but loves back in return!

What are the wounds on your hands,
Sometimes red, a couple of bands,
What happened dear, why is it so,
Oh just my cats, I can't say no!

Baby, today it's in the other one too,
Oh now on your fingers, and it is blue,
Why does this keep happening again,
Okay, Are you sure it doesn't pain?

Ah, now it is the one black,
Is it oil, when hot- did it splash?
Give me your arms, let me take a look,
It's not oil, looks like a hook!

This is my girl, who never let me kiss,
On her neck, nor around her hips,
The cats seem to get this privilege,
What her man can never get in age!

Good night lover!

No matter the age, a girl loves to be put to sleep. Thus, all sweet romance in the world is symbolized by a girl, putting her head over her lover's lap. Although not a singer, my lullaby puts my girl to sleep in a flash!

I want to sing a melody,
Compose a tune quite steady,
Should take you out of here,
Without letting you to steer!

Another world just a little far,
The night will be-many a star,
Where Lillies and Roses blossom,
Only time to hold for a ransom!

You will have the best of sleep,
To a mind that will rest deep,
May it be your tonight darling,
When it's neither cold nor warming!

Hush my girl in the night's lap,
Rock you to a sleepy nap,
Tomorrow will be a better day,
Always, with you, I will stay!

Lullaby Baby

On a day, exhausting, she is rough on the edges and sparky at the corners. A lullaby will not work, and alternate medicine is this poem, which worked its magic on her.

Hush little baby,
Don't say a word,
It's been a long day,
You being a bird!

Over the mountains,
You flew in the sun,
Tired are those wings.
No need to run!

You're back home now,
About to sleep,
Waiting my love,
To your dream you leap!

As I tuck you in,
Kiss you good night,
The angels will now win,
Without a fight!

Sleep little baby,
Apple of my eye,
There is no maybe,
By your side I lie!

She Legend

What is that you call someone, who is perfect, powerful and proud of who they are – a Girl. In being modest, she chooses to disagree with me first, but quickly steps up the pedestal and thanks me for the step!

A woman is a legendary work of art.
Hand drawn and colored by heart,
She is yes, a mirror of your thought,
But, unless there was something you forgot!
She will avenge you if taken granted,
Even if you both stay away parted,
Better be careful about what you say,
Also the stars, the moon and the day!
If you think to learn, yourself the form,
No, Won't let you win anything warm,
Just that your girl will be better calm,
And you will avoid the mines and bombs!
Me, although I think I know her well,
One wrong step and my day will swell,
It's True that I love her back and all,
I am the sole responsible for my cliff fall!

Mesmerizing

From how she moves, to how she speaks, to how she picks and how she treats – everything that is about this girl is a fantasy come true. When such is the case, the only word on the lips is – 'Mesmerizing'!

We all fall in love, true,
Many a times, without clue,
The time and space says,
And lights up our days!

The youngest are sweet,
Fights always being neat,
What do you call each other,
Will we meet again, whether?

Staying away is hard,
Romantic eyes are starred,
Holding hands time and again,
No talks go in vain!

A sweet smile and murmur,
Dirty secrets, careless whisper,
Can't wait to be together,
If only time could stretch like leather!

Don't mind the looks,
Hearts hanging by hooks,
A chocolate and a gentle kiss,
The entire world you may miss!

Seemingly the End

There are some ways that a girl will reject you. And those are the most painful, more than she saying – I want us to part ways. Often leaves me wondering where I went wrong, not to learn better and find another girl, but to fix myself and go back to her!

Till today there were none,
I thought, was my perfect one,
All in the world were flawed,
I, the one they perched and clawed!

They all have their mishaps,
Maybe more than me - perhaps,
Am seeking the impossible?
I pray by sitting in a crucible!

Over, all the fallen leaves here,
I shed more memories and fear,
I stand up now, in front of her;
Confessing my love, my feelings stir!

She is bad in every way - true,
There's no love in her to brew,
Yet, she means to me - my life,
Her absence to me is pain all rife!

Crazy, Stupid Love!

Like I have said earlier, in her love I am nothing short of insane. I start my day with her thought and sleep thinking of how we fought. Between her and I, we know who calls the shots – and with modesty, we give up and fix our knots!

How love my girl, is new,
To me, these things are a-few,
Never, Was I known to be calm,
To her I am everything warm!

She is a rough cat in the morn.
No talks or wishes, no harm,
Now. I do wait for her cool,
Knowing she's inked by some fool!

I am so blessed to know about,
Everything that's her, no doubt,
I cringe, when she tells me how.
People speak to her, in love!

I can now read her silence.
Stay far from her electric fence.
In being all rude, she's my lovely
Holds me up, and I feel dearly!

I love her in ways I can't speak.
Obsessed, is a word very meek.
Baby, without you will burn,
My ashes will love you from the urn!

Let it be just me you're angry with,
Your other world being without a myth,
I'll take all your pain and blame,
Let's talk tonight and settle our game!

How l love my girl, is crazy,
Yes- I've tried not to, not easy,
She's is not just my everything,
To her now, how i helplessly cling!

Cardiac Damage

In search of gems and diamonds, I have dug up my heart – all open. I do it now, even as it pains, to search if there are things I haven't done for my girl yet. From getting her food, to putting her to bed, from driving her to work, and kissing her forehead – I keep discovering new ways of being classy and cheesy.

I am a grown man,
Things in the world I can,
Need nobody rather than,
Trouble from people, I ban!

    I do have self respect,
    In life, a many prospect,
    A few may flag some defect,
    But, nothing short of perfect!

Iam in all meticulous,
Watch my step, never callous,
In things I do, very rigorous,
In a group, the most gregarious!

    I do have a weak spot,
    Although, to hide it,
    I fought, In life, if there - I'm caught,
    One will find me in all wrought!

I am, about this - careful,
Her love it is, I'm plentiful,
I'm in, no matter how dreadful,
She's the only part of my life, fruitful!

I do try my best to part,
Teach myself to build a cart,
Throw at myself a couple dart,
Her smile brings me back to the start!

l am nowhere in her league,
Her beauty makes anyone intrigue,
In her love she will lay siege,
I know howl will fatigue!

I do fear of someone else,
A part for her; how my mind melts,
Knowing every breath of hers,
I cannot survive even with helps!

I am in love, well drenched,
Her talks can make my heart clenched,
Just a touch and I'm quenched,
My love in my heart entrenched!

Tell Tale

Wherever I go, I find a young crowd, asking me about my love and how the spark lives on. The only way to keep loving someone is through memories - out of sight, is out of mind! Watch it, my love birds, if you want to love somebody for your life – create memories and collect artifacts!

Here I tell,
How I love my girl,
On my face I fell,
Touching her curl!

Here I go,
Scared to life,
I kiss her so,
Her fury grows rife?

Here I stand.
Her words l await,
Mute - her pretend,
Did l catch her bait?

Here I wish,
To have her for me,
In pond a many fish,
With me will she be?

Here I pray,
To keep her smiles,
Whatever it takes,
I can walk my miles!

Here I seek,
The girl loved then,
In myself I was weak,
I won't let her count ten!

Typically, Her

Everything about her, from her eyes to her smile is made so perfectly, she is only typical! In giving credit to how she is nothing, but the best under the sun, I always get it back from her, making me run!

My girl wears a smile,
To form, it takes a while,
But when she has it there,
My heart, I will spare!

My girl walks a stroll,
Thoughts are now on roll,
Though I walk aside,
My eyes are always wide!

My girl and her earrings
A Queen bee who stings
She is the beauty in all,
My heart and mind in a brawl!

My girl tucks her hair left,
One sassy and age bereft,
Time and life can only hold,
My love for hen again told!

My girl is very shrewd,
With me, all frank and rude,
She is the goal seek,
My life, she can always peek!

My girl is just everything.
The only one to whom I cling,
There exists no self now,
My hands can only take a bow!

Spiritual Love

Some say love is divine, some may say it is pleasure – in all that is said and meant, to love someone is an experience. Its entirety never contained. There is no end of the world that one can reach, and such is love – with the vastness of the Universe!

To love a girl is divine,
Drenched in her thought,
In counting one to nine,
At ten, she's the only sought!

To wake up every morn,
Dreaming of just a day,
While her picture I adorn,
Wondering what she may say!

To meet her later is a wish,
Wondering what she may wear,
Her boundless beauty is a bliss,
Her absence I cannot bear!

To love her more than life,
Something I never could guess,
Could she be my wife,
That would be so much less!

To wait for her again,
Is a sweet pain so dear,
She is now a stubborn stain,
All my heart, I smear!

To think what is that in her,
That makes me fly above,
Drops of love, like honey were,
She had rained on me, how!

To be loved by her, a boon,
How I pray for those days back,
Walk along under the moon,
Close to her without slack!

She, just she!

When the person you love is beyond all words, language and poetry are subtle and a meaningless verse. The one who loves can only understand – what the codes mean, and how your lover will stand to reprimand!

My girl, I cannot stop talking about,
She's the most beautiful, without doubt,
When she wears her smile, even a pout,
So, we fight and she throws me out!

My girl, is just everything I ever need,
She's my love and pain, though good deed,
All in common, she is just my creed,
Touch my hair, I'll be her loyal steed!

My girl, makes no effort to dress,
Pajamas and others, her hair is a mess,
Nails are trimmed, no polish to guess,
Her being with me is the way she'll bless!

My girl, plays it very shy and coy,
She Ties her hair, lets it down, oh boy!
Hoping she'll love me, I'm in all joy,
And her gift is not the one at Troy!

My girl, is now more than my life,
Loving this beauty, I can take in a knife,
Although our fights often grow rife,
To win her, my heart and mind in a strife!

When in life -

It was after almost a decade that I even learnt that a man would try, only when in love. The rest of the kind will choose to give up and live the life of half-dead, while sulking in disappointment or trying to renounce the pleasure of being in Love!

Only when you love a woman,
You'll know how to be,
Even in hunger, you're starving,
How the world will see,
She may be your life's villain,
Makes you just believe,
In her angels and your demon,
Oh you're so naive!

Only when you miss your girl,
You'll know how it feels,
You start dreaming of her curl,
All eyes on her heels,
Your heart will now- throb and whirl,
Awaiting her on kneels,
In her oyster, she's a Pearl,
Realize what she means!

Only when she's not around,
You'll know who she is,
A tad little less than all abound,
In her heart, you lease,
Give all you have, on the mound,
And ask her gently, please,
She comes closer, without a sound,
Killing all your peace!

Only when you've not given up,
And by saying no lies,
If you're lucky, may fill your cup,
Asking no premise,
You will then know, about her hiccup,
Naughty girl in disguise,
By now all your lines are a pickup,
For her, you'll have no vice!

Have you ever?

To love an object is very different – never can reach the apex or epitome of what is meant! One will need the company of another, not just in care and affection, but mutual love, together!

Have you ever loved someone,
That they are your day,
Who always make you run,
Like being chased by a ray,
Who, when is not around,
Makes your lips say,
Darling, I am feeling deep drowned,
Without you, in the abyss I will lay!

Have you ever been with that one,
Who defines the world to you,
That one who is the morning sun,
In their absence, nothing you do,
Like how the forests will vanish,
When there is no rain,
And like how the silver will tarnish,
With none to hold, all in vain!

Have you ever held someone,
Tight and close, and yet gentle,
Like how a mother cat would run,
Holding her kitten, by neck - subtle,
Fire, waiting to burn you down,
Yet your love is so soft,
Throw away both your crown,
A kiss will blow you both aloft!

Have you ever cared for that one,
About everything they do,
Whether its all trouble or fun,
To know, what's around and who,
If you're not going to be there,
How will things not be blue,
Why would your love want to go,
Into a something they have no clue!

Have you ever loved someone,
Knowing that they don't,
Even when they point you a gun,
To trust their trigger won't,
To your pet, you are the only one,
It may never say it loud,
I love my girl in my jokes and pun,
Her smile, makes me proud!

Marine Love

This was a poem that my girl loved the most! In my mind I imagined she kissing the page, reading through each phrase. In the end she said, I have done my best yet, and my next poems should only fly higher than this one has flown!

Through all the monstrous nights,
The waves and ravaging seas,
She tossed and pitched, the tides,
Not giving her breathing means,
Though it was all water around,
She begged for mercy please,
The water to consume her bound,
At her agony, nature did tease!

Through the dark of the night,
There sailed another tug aside,
In mooring her close to sight,
The seas didn't seem so wide,
Her rolls now stopped therein,
And the pitches slowly damped,
What the tug did was to pin,
Herself to its starboard clamped!

Through all this, nature learnt itself,
Not to poke this ship hard,
It took only a tiny tug to help,
Can stand tall as her guard,
Bring it on loud, yelled the tug,
Are you now scared of me,
She's never alone, dare you bug,
Not the rock, nor the sea!

Through this story I may narrate,
What one may need at most,
Even if nature uses you as a bait,
Just one soul, you sail to coast,
All the pains have passed straight,
The dirt you have gathered and shoved,
In all sadness and heavy weight,
Her heart etched - "She was Loved!"

Suspense

Love is the congregation of all confusion and uncertainty. Some say they use the stars to predict the next steps, and some others believe in their actions. Irrespective of what you believe or not, the important part of being in love is to know when your lover can't figure how to say things out loud!

There is something, Hidden out there,
Often a sharp sting, would rather not dare,
Fear, it does ring, I will never fare,
Even if I have a wing, those winds will tear!
    Like flashes of light, Passing in bands,
    Sound without sight, Life pulled in strands,
    What if it is all right, Maybe helping hands,
    Why in my mind bright, Would I wield my wands?
Yet it never fails, in hogging my mind,
If she opens her sails,To the winds, she may bind,
A shore full of nails, Nobody there kind,
What if there it hails, Me, she can't find?
    Why is my girl, On this adventure,
    Into the rough whirl, A world immature,
    What do I hurl, Wrong in my stature,
    Loves me through her curl, And runs me a lecture!

Yes, she loves me, Like just a friend,
But none there like me, I am her end,
Everything about me, Her life I do bend,
If it is just me, Her rules, she will mend!
    Her "No" is just, What I always hear,
    Never deny her gust, even if she's not near,
    Hold her fist, not to hurt her back, dear,
    She'll shower a mist, Her love crystal clear!

Bird out

I am the fireman in life, although my assignment is only to put out her fires. I stand ground and prepared, for the needs of my girl, from being lost to scheming someone's fate. For such responsibilities in life – which I earned over the years – I now watch her sail in high tide. I am given clear instructions, not to bother her! Worried, every moment, I stand here with my sword facing the earth!

Day tomorrow, my nestling will fly,
Not too far, but across the winds high,
She was always ready, just not me,
It takes a lot to let her soar, and see!

She needs this and we both know,
Yet it aches a bit, it shouldn't so,
I miss her already, just so it is,
Her mind is steady, a cool breeze!

All I want is her happy smile,
If not me, even so otherwise,
Whatever it takes, to see my girl laugh,
Candies and cakes, a little more than half!

I know she'll be back soon,
Knowing she'll be safe,
It's my soul that misses her,
Through the night, keeps me awake!

As I count the days to a week,
Waiting for you to give me a peek,
What all you did and how was the day,
I'll be waiting darling, have a peaceful stay!

Tomorrow will be better

On a day, which is not so bright – and all the aspects of life seem futile, it is only the beauty of a woman which can remove the veil that has engulfed your mind. As for me, I need her face and her voice – and the entire universe will become a better place to live, in a flash of a moment!

Save it for the rainy day,
Not a usual thing to say,
While I being drenched and lay,
Don't you dock, stay at bay!

The lighthouse is no more lit,
Harrowing waves, now they hit,
Not my plans, nor my wit,
Can pull me out, of this deep pit!

None of you can even fathom,
Your futile guesses, all random,
No, this does not happen often,
Only now, I am brash and brazen!

Yes, my moon has slipped today,
Through in dark, I hope to stay,
Her supportive lover, far away,
It will never be a fair play!

The only thing that now holds,
Is her smile, a few rare jolts,
Her endless beauty, sunk in my folds,
A gentlemen, myself in moulds!

Today, is just my strike one,
Days ahead, are more to come,
How many more should I now sum,
In missing her, I end up sad and bum!

Save it all, just for now,
Tomorrow, you may wonder how,
The days passed in all of love,
To hold her hand, I need no cove!

Obsessed

Obsession is a bad thing, only when it affects somebody other than you. For lesser mortals like me, it helps me live on the cloud of fantasy and the pains of life appear absent. These may sound like the words of an addict, and I admit, she is my only addiction, and I am proud to be called so.

You may now call me obsessed,
About the sole thing that matters today,
In many ways, I am just blessed,
I get an ounce of love, floating my way,
My only pain lies in things guessed,
Though there is not much I have to say,
It all ends when she comes dressed,
Now the world will get, only my nay!

You may go on and ask me many,
Mundane life with nothing great to tell,
The only fun in life, if there is any,
Is about my girl and her cast spell,
There is something in being uncanny,
Everyone guessing where's my bell,
You'll only get white lies for a penny,
If not being cornered to hear my yell!

You may wonder, how I am any good,
Little does it bother me, about you,
I will pass you all, under my hood,
It wouldn't matter, in life what you do,
Long as she is smiling, you will be stood,
None here will get any clue,
I will hold her hand and stick like wood,
Who here cares if you are red or blue!

Still ....

Some moments that I spend with my girl are very special. It defies all laws of a relationship, and yet we are a couple who are together. We split up asking each other for some space and time – only realizing that the rest of the world is non–existent to both of us. So, on many occasions, I am stuck on a single note from a Banjo – over days and weeks!

Still wondering if it was a dream,
Dressed in all white, as is cream,
Standing by the heavy curtains beige,
In a flash, my heart is under siege,
Legs crossed, a little barely so,
A rose gold watch, makes itself a bow,
Poked shrug around her shoulders,
Her lovely smile is what makes wonders!

Still thinking, will I ever stand there,
My left hand over her shoulder, I dare,
In my arm, she will look well seated,
Before the flash, my kiss - she'll be greeted,
Her silver pendant chooses to dance,
A chain that adorns her, I stare! not glance,
The picture, now etched deep inside,
My soul is wounded, deep and wide!

Still shocked at the sight of flowers,
She stood there like a white rose,
The other small ones waiting for hours,
Her click once, they could stop to pose,
I turned blank looking at this beauty,
Not sure how many around watched,
Fell in love again, like it is my duty,
My memory about her is now notched!

Still there, posing by a marble lion,
You know? maybe she was Narnia's scion,
Unsure now, how not to be jealous,
When my girl holds its chin, callous!
I can be her pet, if she wants,
Maybe she watches me and my stance,
This girl, I will let her tame me,
If she can agree to me, calling us We!

The earth

She brings me my warmth, my breath and my desire, makes me home in the comfort of her, when my time is dire. She knows when I am thirsty and desperate, even without me saying a word, through my eyes – when my tears decorate. She is everything a guy misses in life – the only thing she is not, is my wife!

It is said about the might seas,
Without the shores, they are never at ease,
They may toss a vessel across,
May as well roar and shred a blade of grass,
Often, they wreck havoc out there,
To the souls who challenge them and dare,
It is only near the ends they are,
Calm and pristine, from everyone afar!

It is known from time unbound,
The mountains stand the wind from ground,
The taller they are, earth they span,
Softer they become, and people they ban,
Lesser mortals, try to scale them again,
Pulling on an avalanche, more stories they pen,
For the mountains, they seldom care,
A blanket of trees, they flaunt and wear!

It is much spoken, among the elders,
Never play with fire, let alone the splinters,
A burn wound takes time to heal,
It takes longer for anything to feel,
As fire it is, it does decimate,
Anything that even tries to hold state,
But the inferno does need a wick,
And to keep that fire, I am the stick!

It is often talked about the thunder,
Lighting and rumble, continues to wander,
Electric, they call the storm,
It may not always be dreamy, but warm,
Thus my girl, is mighty as above,
Me, the object who does nothing but love,
Just like nature, she is the resplendent,
To circle her now, I can only be abundant!

Her Trip

My vanilla cheesecake chooses to travel on a few occasions. I do not ask her if I can join, to let her hold her peace. Like in movies, I watch her, while she talks – while my mind keeps yelling, just say 'Yes, you can come and join my walk'. And when she says goodbye, even for a short while, I start reeling in the cold of her absence.

Once her trip is finalized,
The rest of my world stays ostracized,
And as her days start closing by,
My heart and mind start questioning why,
Following are days anxious,
Everything said and done are viscous,
Then comes the nights of despair,
Wondering why my life is beyond repair!

On her day of travel it is,
Excited for her, I start to miss,
Want to know her every step,
Each moment my heart would've wept,
I still don't get it, why is it so,
I am crippled and can never let her go,
When she is now in airplane mode,
My heart starts breaking in every node!

Once she's landed, I do sigh,
Tracked her flight like a pilot guy,
Did she get her cab ride to,
Anybody around, if so who?
Check-in to her hotel, is she tired,
Turn off all lights, check if the room's wired,
Lie down for a while my darling now,
When should I wake you, where and how?

On the mark, I'll get you ready,
Everything okay? And are you steady?
Share where you are, let me see,
Take some pics, with you let me be,
Nobody now, should cause trouble,
I'm with my girl, I'll smash you to rubble,
Go around baby, have a nice day,
Little murmur, but I'll stay away!

Once all her days have now passed,
I can't be more excited, emotions amassed,
When darling, is your flight back,
The days of loneliness have well stacked,
Can I pick you from the airport,
Waiting for you to let me in your fort,
When my girl is back after a trip,
Shouldn't bother her, if I shouldn't want a whip!

Beauty beyond words

What do I call this girl so beautiful? Anything I say or add would be a futile desperate attempt to talk about something so abstract. Everything about her is just perfect, from her smile to her desire. Superlative and exemplary are words that do not stand to mean what my girl is, however she's seen!

She is the most beautiful,
For not just me, but the world,
Her presence makes one feel soulful,
Even with her hair uncurled,
The smile that floors anyone,
Adults and children alike,
She stands near me, I am done,
All men around, feel a pike!

She has those wide eyes,
Dark and deep as a forest's sky,
With brows shaped like a slice,
Watching, a day – I can lie,
Her long nose ending sharp,
And the sliver of an above lip,
Time with her is always a warp,
Ends of her smile, a delicate tip!

She flaunts the skin of gold,
Not for the lesser mortals,
Holding high her dresses' fold,
Walks into my hearts' portals,
It is here that she vanishes fast,
I wonder when she left,
She tells me about going past,
Through my heart's gorge and rift!

She owns a class and body,
How gracefully she does carry,
Her call awaiting ready,
A day to make her my quarry,
Her toes are those of magic,
I only get to imagine,
Praying my love not to end tragic,
I will welcome committing a sin!

Girl Down!

The sickness of my girl is more horrible to me than her. Although she suffers through the discomfort, it is I – who is stuck between rocks, unable to be with her and take care. While I want to be close to her through her bad days, I know that is not somewhere I can stay for long and she wouldn't let me belong!

At times when she's not her best,
My care, seems to be put to test,
Staying this far is good, never,
Cold and cough, some mild fever,
She pulls herself within the shell,
Seldom speaker, now a silenced bell,
Here, as I wait my turn to meet,
A sight of her, will tear my sad sheet!

Over a hundred times on a usual day,
Her thoughts' a cushion on which I lay,
Is on days like these I am worried,
Of changing winds, everything hurried,
If I can only be by her side,
Hot water, pills and stay her aide,
Not as much of love and romance,
Ensuring her health is not left to chance!

Through the day she's my sleepalina,
Over the week she looks way more leaner,
Staying apart in love is hard,
When you want to nurture her, a ward,
Whatever I am, to her is weird,
To talk to me or be seen with me, feared,
Even in desperate times I'm to stay afar,
This hurts so bad, though none's at par!

I haven't heard from her in a day,
Hopeless things my mind is up to say,
Maybe she did fall very sick,
What if around, there's not even a stick,
That day when she fainted alone,
To play, I was happily picking up a stone,
Please tell me now, what's going on,
My reflexes aren't poor, though a little worn!

My lover, now is awfully weak,
Praying for a while, my hands in a creak,
Twenty four on the clock, is very long,
My throats dry with over a hundred song,
Darling, you'll be fine very soon,
For you I'll wait under the bright moon,
Whatever is so troubling my baby,
If I could only take it from you, maybe!

One thing and the other

The story of the Ying and the Yang, the positive and the negative, the love and hate, the desire and renunciation is alive in philosophy from the history of time. What is intriguing about "Us" is that we complement each other and find a good thing (at least me) in what the other does. Thus, my love for my girl is always growing!

A thing that burns and one to quench,
That one to fall and another winch,
Far across the magnetic poles,
So in life are our mutual roles!

A thing that seldom talks in a day,
Another finds it a struggle to stay,
The former wants to let things be,
The later eagerly waiting to see!

A thing that loves but cannot tell,
The other with love, keeps ringing a bell,
Put together they're just perfect,
A clear diamond with no defect!

A thing that hates a question second,
One wrong move, will gracefully fend,
The other fears this to its soul,
Collecting all tears in a crying bowl!

A thing that gave up the world in past,
Nothing mattered as time flew fast,
The other now is beyond repair,
Fell head first in all despair!

A thing about this couple be said,
Doesn't matter the color blue or red,
Without the other they cease to work,
Like the prongs apart on a tuning fork!

Homewards

In your good times or bad, find that one who is strong to hold you. And if they hold you through strong winds, they are your saviors, and are made for your life. Although I fear that my love may part, someday maybe – but her presence is bliss today and all future to be!

I was far away from books and pen,
There was a guy who lived across then,
Who had not one, but many a crash,
Cared for nothing and awfully brash,
Met a girl in pain with a broken heart,
Who walked around with many a dart!
Both their worlds had hurt them scraping,
They both had a hole quite gaping!

In deep waters she slowly drowned,
He kept wandering hoping to be found,
Not in words nor in this earthly realm,
Could they seek the other in any psalm,
But so was what it seemed conspired,
Over time and space together admired,
Took a small step towards the other,
Into a plait they both tied a tether!

What appeared to be shocking and new,
Wore the beauty of a morning dew,
Head over heels they fell in love,
All the looming skies, cleared above,
A peaceful rain of cold drops followed,
The world of romance now swallowed,
The man now became a caring lover,
Healed her wounds and moved her cover!

Though the story goes far and beyond,
Unlikely two can seamlessly bond,
What matters most isn't who you are,
Where you're from, even if not at par,
When life shows up with the soul mate,
Care less about the others and fate,
Hold their hands and start moving towards,
Home, that you will build together, leewards!

What if she

In her thoughts when I am about to sleep, I slip into these loops where she is somebody else, and I am by her side. Quite amazing how I do love her, irrespective of who she is in all those hundred possible ways! Yet, she is none of them, and neither am I. Just neck deep in love, that goes beyond all worlds!

If she was an officer,
Fighting crime for us all,
Troubles, theft, fights and stir,
Powered up, yet my doll,
Come home tired chasing loot,
Sit back now, cross the wall,
Let me get my playing flute,
All music and love may fall!

If she may be was a lawyer,
Standing up for truth and just,
Mince the bad and put on fire,
Ask some more and slowly test,
I would drive her back now,
Sit back, relax and get some rest,
Let me calm your air above,
On my lap in our nest!

If she was doctor yet,
Saving lives and relieve pain,
As a subject I'd have met,
On her bed, kept me lain,
For all service she'd have kept,
Her leisure time and all her gain,
I'd well keep our home swept,
Free from trouble and any stain!

If she was an astronaut,
Finding stars and flying away,
Stay classified and secrets a lot,
Awaiting her, my heart will sway,
I will love the making of a hero,
Standing behind and watching her wave,
She shoots to the moon an arrow,
Learning myself how to behave!

If she was a professor,
Teaching everyone beyond age,
Libraries then named after her,
My girl would create an adage,
In time, thinking of how we were,
Picking up our live's image,
Bookmarks made of colourful feather,
Her Nobel, I would dress her back stage!

My girl now is an engineer,
Her thought and wisdom at her best,
In this world nothing is fear,
For I take care of her rest,
To your calling, I stand here,
Wherever you are, trough or crest,
In my life, you are always near,
With folded hands, at your behest!

Your Savior

Give her all reins, you mortal man – she is the only one who loves you and can! In your lows and your highs, she gives up her wishes and sacrifice. She makes you call your place as "Home", she is all God, without her you are alone!

It may be your everyday hue,
Or just when the moon turns blue,
You may have little or no clue,
Or just stuck like a rat to glue,
May have to stand in a long queue,
Life is all harsh, we know that's true,
When you love a girl, you're due,
Know that you are her striking cue!

God has made her rightly so,
One can never try saying no,
Even if you do make her bow,
You will always reap what you sow,
Kneads you into a perfect dough,
You'll end up having nowhere to go,
Where to run, you wouldn't know,
In the end, she's your only tow!

Know that when she says okay,
She's got a plan, don't you play,
You may hurt her and make her lay,
She'll always put her heart on a tray,
In asking you to go away and stay,
Would want you far - just for a day,
She may hurt and push to say,
From today you better be at bay!

That girl now - is the chosen one,
On a cloudy day, she'll be your sun,
Don't leave her side, when there's none,
Choose no talk, yourself you stun,
Never say yes when she says it's done,
Stand there brave, facing her gun,
If you've loved her without a pun,
If not today, tomorrow you'll stand won!

In Retrospective

Often, we take things, we have for granted, and try to live the moment to our best. If only we know that we may never see this moment again, our perspective of life changes to beauty everywhere. I miss those times when I had everything in my arms, and not realizing what I may miss in the future. I could have been so much better!

It is true that life is unfair,
To love someone being all bare,
Often frozen and stuck in a stare,
People and others you don't care!

As of me, I've always truly loved,
Wishes and thoughts are yet shoved,
The lawn of my desires I keep mowed,
To my girl - no trouble, I stay vowed!

We were a couple, I knew her least,
All I gave was raw love and yeast,
Now when I know her well and most,
We're not together and I'm a ghost!

Times never matched for her and I,
Should've now been together and lie,
Now I regret why we said goodbye,
Praying to the universe to make us tie!

I now know what makes her smile,
Frown and curse, what makes her rile,
Thinking of the past, for over a while,
My list of mistakes is as long as Nile!

How I wish we were now lovers,
Building our life like young beavers,
Talking about the world, both averse,
If only in time, I could travel reverse!

I still hold her soft hands in mine,
Once a while, I love you, to nine,
I will walk along your perfume line,
Caress your arms as we slowly dine!

Maybe I will wake up to a dawn,
By my side, holding me like a pawn,
Us both, watching all time gone,
Blue sky above and the dew kissed lawn!

An Impossible Trek

At times we sign up for things we aren't sure of yet. Although the summit is what we seek, the trek will drain us and make us weak. For having trekked on this path a few times, I know what is waiting for me up there. Even so, on some days, the exhaustion makes me write like this.

What in this world do I seek,
In crying every night, awfully meek,
Stuck like a fish in the falcons' beak,
I struggle for breath and blood I leak!

Philosophy and life, I seem to like,
As each day and time, pick up their pike,
Rain down clouds, go on and strike,
A volcanic mountain, I've picked to hike!

I've passed the trails and open lands,
Gravel and rocks and loose sands,
My feet are sore and wounds are bands,
I now crawl the earth by pulling hands!

In God at times, I have lost my trust,
In all the pain, I curse myself first,
The air is dry and high is my thirst,
As each day passes, I grovel to worst!

On a good day, I am, at best - fed,
Though chained down with weights of lead,
I can hear everything that is said,
Let me run away from hell, instead!

I may wake up to a day - an Angel,
Walk around with happiness in a satchel,
Someone, rescuing me from the kennel,
Breaking my chains on a heavy anvil!

Now this is only, all but a rant,
I was the one who ran far and pant,
In waiting for my turbid life to decant,
I will emerge from the caves like a mutant!

The dark of her eyes!

It took me a while to understand that it's her eyes that captivates me when I sit across from her, lost in thought. As she talks and asks questions, I'm drawn into the conversation, yet my lips seem to whisper endlessly how much I love her. All the while, it's those mesmerizing eyes that hold me spellbound, keeping me lost throughout.

I see something in those deep eyes,
At that gaze, melts all my vice,
Lost, chanting 'I love you', thrice
On her fingers I'm the rolling dice,
For this girl I can pay my hearts price,
Just her look, I can dance on thin ice!

Yet those eyes can hold my breath,
The black in them are our shibboleth,
When she's around I will chase death,
Hold her hands to a tree underneath,
A day without her, I'm deprived of meth,
Falling now into the dark infinite depth!

Those eyes glow now in her anger,
Something I did, again a dagger,
Let her take out her wrath and fire,
I know I will be back, all dire,
We both know how this will get better,
By me not uttering a word or letter!

Back to her brows, a plateau sharp,
I dive through calm into her warp,
A safe place she is, even in the dark,
She holding me, I will fight a shark,
Walking away, it will peel my bark,
On my heart, her name is the only mark!

Only twice her eyes open wide,
When she's excited, I'm in a glide,
Other is when, I should run and hide,
Don't know who's the piper - here pied,
A cat she is, to catch my when I've lied,
She never asks, but I always abide!

Someday

We all need a 'Someday'—a moment to nurture our hopes, weave our dreams, and truly live our lives. Perhaps one day, my 'Someday' will come, when she and I will be together once more.

Some live a life is across time,
Generations and history in line,
Many stories where couples whine,
Their lives and ours do rhyme!

A few through the word of mouth,
Few others that went awfully south,
Either of the lovers, how all devout,
The couple lived with a broken spout!

Yet the beating hearts are all divine,
Even when one of them in a ravine,
If not anybody, time itself malign,
For the lovers could never align!

The people around could never lift,
Trying their best to cause a rift,
While the world continues to drift,
Emotions bled and dried very swift!

It may be after all these thoughts,
Either erased the love to dots,

As the other with life in knots,
Filling all the feelings in pots!
                    Maybe someday we both together,
                    Hold hands and face the stormy weather,
                    The fire around may burn us to leather,
                    Our hearts will always be on a tether!
Then on, we both will be a new couple,
Who would have survived a life's ripple,
Our story would be the syrup of maple,
We would get the embrace of our people!

The wild

Forests and wildlife are among the most intriguing places on Earth, revealing both their harshness and their beauty. As is the couple I'm writing about, an unexpected pair—one that defies convention but exists harmoniously. They may seem mismatched, yet they belong together in their own extraordinary way.

There's once lived an unusual pair,
A mighty tiger and a grizzly bear,
Both met saying life's very unfair,
Their trust and love in a bad tear,
There hardly was anything to share,
In due course they started to care,
They started climbing uphill in a dare,
Warning each other of the open snare!

Over time they grew fond and close,
Holding each other, together they rose,
A little love they fed each other, a dose,
Like a snail, in time, ended their woes,
Now a couple, they would proudly pose,
With affection they would kiss the nose,
They now spoke to the other their vows,
Dreamt on how to home their house!

Though yet they didn't belong together,
A feline and the untamed, not a feather,
The couple would make the world go gather,
Their lives and fears, to run away rather,
Now they spanned the forests and farther,
Around the trees and streams meander,
The fauna shouting, made for each other,
In all the follies, these two blamed neither!

A few now watched the couple in hands,
Evil eyes cast and they spilt in bands,
The tiger intact, but the bear in strands,
Their love shattered down to the glands,
Yet they couldn't now part on the lands,
The bear kept visiting their posing stands,
Seemed stuck in the marshy wetlands,
While the winds tore its fur by flying sands!

The tiger suffered behind the closed door,
Bracing itself up for something more,
You love better, when apart, says folklore,
Their love would hence become the core,
Of life, teaching us love - how to pour,
And build a stronghold for patience to store,
Reminiscing, what they ate and wore,
Doesn't matter who, love is always - galore!

Story of a Day

She is extraordinary in every way, and I could never tire of writing about her. With just one small step, she can make my entire world tremble and bloom. Whether it's the simple grace of her movements or the depth of her care, she turns the mundane into the magical. If anyone could be truly celestial, it would be none else than – My Girl.

Once she gave me a watch to wear,
Shine and a lustre, enough to glare,
A dial so deep and inviting a stare,
With nobody now will I ever share!

Made for someone, to adorn with pride,
Enough to lift my mood in every stride,
You guessed it right, I now smile wide,
How I do follow her orders and abide!

She only took, not a day but four,
Through the options and finally ashore,
A master timepiece from days of yore,
Just a relic for her man to adore!

How she's troubled and cannot say,
With him she should stand at bay,
Wear it with white, maybe someday,
He made it cream, in his own way!

All knowing it was white she wanted,
Without one yet, he stays haunted,
Another way he screwed up, counted,
Mental fingers at him - now pointed!

In a few days maybe, he'll wear it right,
Hope it'll be perfect to invite a bite,
Her mind going on a repeat to cite,
You're missing him, in dark and light!

The Duo

This one is for her and the special one she nurtures. She mentioned that this one is in her list of favorites.

Somewhere far in the tropical greens,
A cub danced to its whimsical dreams,
The mother keeping a watch closely,
A few paces behind on thatch, wisely,
Although there is nothing here to fear,
There's not much trust, none's dear,
She can never barely catch a wink,
Let alone the peace, can she ever sink!

She rests her eyes between her paws,
Watching him pull the rocks with claws,
The wounds on her back, tries to forget,
Along with the nights of her lonely regret,
Although the cub knows it all through,
It's age and mind let's it cope from blue,
The mother sighs and tries to move on,
As the cub chases her back and clings on!

Sees there is something by the bushes,
She sniffs the air and tries her rushes,
Her baby is now her only goal to save,
Ready to fight the world on a wave,

Holds the cub by its neck and lashes,
Leaps across the rocks avoiding clashes,
Now she has gained quite some ground,
Lays him down, a little peace now she found!

The days fell through to years and more,
Cub, no longer, he has a mighty roar,
A young male now he can find his prey,
She stands back and counts her grey,
With each strand talking life's lesson,
Thankful she bows down for all blessing,
Watching over the little one now cross,
The bounds of her love, stepping on moss!

After many years, she is now calm,
To enjoy the sun and the day's warm,
There is nothing much to look and advice,
She's nurtured a cub, clean off all vice,
Stretches now with a snort on a rock,
Keeps her eyes looking, just for the clock,
What can make the Queen more happy,
Than her awesome cub, just so peppy!

Monumental

She is the one who can shine my mind, and the one who lets me whine behind! In everything she does, she is only the best – for I cannot see beyond her eyes. To such a person I write this poem – she will most probably, not understand.

There is a castle atop the hill,
Built by some greats at their will,
It may have been white some time,
Of what remains few traces of lime,
A family may have lived here then,
Rooms too big for a count of ten,
There it stands, behind the pines,
In the mornings, the glass do shine.

Guess it went without any care,
When all moved out with their pair,
Stands tall now some masonry,
To get inside, it feels cold and awry,
A few years ago, someone went there,
To search for any treasure and dare,
They did find a cellar sealed,
To snap it open, some wood they peeled.

When they all could get inside,
They found a place dark and wide,
It looked like as if the whole floated,
A wooden ladder with paint coated,
They walked around and were shocked,
Not a piece of wood there docked,
Running out of there thinking haunted,
The seconds to minutes, time they counted.

They found a book and pen in a trunk,
Stained but water, and that room stunk,
It was a one barely half written,
The writing looked of someone quitting,
It seemed like a story of how the castle,
In its prime was all colorful dazzle,
The man who built it for his lover,
Shaped the castle like her flower.

How this man always wished to defy,
Stood to build a castle and glorify,
Love for his woman needs nothing to stand,
The stones would speak itself with sand,
Cellar would have nothing to hold,
The stones and wood would've then told,
To glue together, one would need love,
Like nothing else, just like from above.

A River

All beauty of the world is always addressed as a girl. From the river that nurtures, to a ship that sails – all that is too beautiful to express is termed as a woman. Maybe there is a reason to it, that a woman can only be known to the inner heart and words are a futile effort of humankind, to address something as much as her!

This poem is special, as I concealed her identity in a river. While she caught the subtle references, I misled her through the strong currents. This piece was good enough for her to term as Awesome.

Through dense forests,
Gorges and the valleys,
A gentle stream starts,
Picking up, it marches,
Down with the pebbles,
The loose soil embarks,
A new line of life,
A River thus is born!

She picks up friends,
And adds to her might,
What seems mundane,
To the human eye,

As she carves rocks,
Marking her path,
A new line of beauty,
A River thus is wide!

Dancing all in grace,
She's now in her rapids,
A boat tries to race,
Which turns and tosses,
Pushes a log heavy,
Down by a fall,
A new line of might,
A River thus is formed!

Spans the meadows wide,
In her, new lives thrive,
Although calm above,
Her current is as thrice,
Bowing down is the way,
She knows her means well,
A new line of peace,
A River thus has no vice!

Blends with the ocean,
She walked all the way,
Calm with no emotion,
Like she waited no day,
Shares a careless whisper,
With the salty waters,
A new line of hope,
A River thus is ripe!

In all her way along,
She never returns to past,
What she's abandoned,
Finds its way to rot,
The lives she carries,
Can only be content,
A new line of water,
A River thus is life!

If she floods ever,
That's just man's folly,
As she changes course,
You wait for her next rally,
She's gone for good,
The rocks weather in heat,
A new line of pain,
A River thus is gone!

Carved a new path,
She sways in pride,
New lands are made,
And more lives abide,
You can only seek,
Her merciful bless,
A new line of her stride,
To a River, thus you pray!

Love is always incomplete.
As if, it was otherwise,
The world wouldn't have any misery!

P.S - I love you

To you, who I adore..
22 Sep 2024

This is the actual post script of the book. I am not addressing this to you, nor signing this because I want this message to live in the ether forever. Just like the bygone era of throwing messages in the bottle, here is my effort to reach your shores with something to say. This book may not be well appreciated by you anymore - although you are the muse to every letter in print.

You have all your engines on, full steam ahead, as you leave port. The tug I was, is no more to function to your needs. The waters are deep now and you float fine like a knife on butter. I will not follow you now, for you have a new fine captain, I trust. I pray for all the good in the world to escort you on your voyage, waving my hat and flag, seeing you go.

Having written over 200 poems, all about you and I'm happy you've read them all - or that I've made you read. I can only be grateful to your abundance of patience and love that you have showered all while. For those brief years I was with you, was the golden era of my life and I will pen it to a book towards my end. And if you will visit me in my passing, may I beg you to carry this book with you?

Now I wish, if you are holding this book and reading this page, if you will leave the impression of your lips - here, my life's purpose would have been met.

Apologies for making this as cheesy as it may get. If I will ever get to have you back in my life, whenever, wherever, however……... here, I have no more words to pen, as a pair of tears are rollIng down my eyes.. Sayonara..

Always yours,

NOTES:

About the Author

In a world of constant change, what significance does a name hold? This question resonates with Sree, a debut poet stepping into the literary realm. Known for sharing his personal poems with his beloved, Sree has ventured into the expansive world of literature, encouraged by his sweetheart's gentle nudge.

As he navigates the labyrinthine streets of a bustling city, his bumper sticker reads, "The less told, the less known, the less is thought and the lesser shown." Time may be fleeting and patience scarce, but Sree believes that love is the answer and care is the reason. He asserts that life on earth is inconceivable without some form of love.

In what he says that the limits of love are boundless, there are only more ways to share your heart than there already are. It is only through art and literature that the true essence of life can be experienced, and the longing felt - making us humans capable of understanding a little more about love than all else, writes Sree.

www.ingramcontent.com/pod-product-compliance
Lightning Source LLC
LaVergne TN
LVHW090048160826
845672LV00015B/1607

9798895560112

which confirms an individual's identity. After confirmation that my clone is the most wanted Don, he would be the one to go through trials and tribulation and then the inevitable persecution. Once he is hanged, I would be a free person.

The Don notices Denzongpa still looking at the screen behind, "Are you with me?" he asks.

Denzongpa's expression sour at the sight of Mr. Kher. A cocktail of jealousy, hatred, and disgust is evident on his face. "I had lost my scholarship because of him. He was my batch mate," he says, recollecting his college days." Then, bringing down his gaze towards the Don, he says, "Yes, he is genius but would never be our partner once he comes to know the purpose for which his formula of DNA Identical cloning would be used."

"He is a human being," the Don says pulling a cigar from the case and tapping on it. "He could be bought, requested, or forced."

"That man would never fall for force or temptation," Denzongpa gives him the light.

"We have to have that formula by hook or crook," says the Don, releasing a cloud of smoke.

CAREFREE COMMERCE LIFE

Ranbir enters Elphinstone college. Elphinstone college, one of the oldest colleges of Mumbai, having gothic structure, has faculties like Arts, Science and Commerce under one roof. It also provides hostel facilities to its outstation students. Its campus is buzzing with activities. It's a kind of a mini New York City. Break dancing at one end, tattooing at another. The canteen is more frequented than class lectures. The corridors are almost a fashion show ramp. It's a total hang out spot.

But today the environment looks a little tensed. Ranbir goes to the notice board, displayed in the college corridor. He runs his finger over the list of A.T.K.T. Suddenly it stops at – Sushant passed with 3 kt's. Excited, he searches for his own name. Ranbir is thrilled and pounces the buttons on his mobile.

"Sushant, where are you!", Ranbir screams into his mobile, caring a damn for the classmates around who have now covered their ears.

"Sushant is busy, call later," Raman answers from the other end.

"Tell him we both have passed with only 3 K.T's!", Ranbir exclaims, happiness evident in his tone.

"You are 25 minutes late in reporting," Raman replies with a hint of teasing. "Anyways, I can't risk disturbing him now"

A lady professor notices Ranbir's excitement of having passed with 3. KT's. "Won't you celebrate"? she asks.

"Yes Mam, plans on!", Ranbir replies with an innocent grin.

"SHAMELESS" are the parting words of Miss Sinha.

"*Khud ke figure ka pata nahi, aur aai hai geography sikhane,*" Ranbir says behind her back.

A nerd passing-by rectified Ranbir, "Excuse me, she is our Economics professor, Miss Sinha. We don't even have geography as our subject in our college."

Ranbir gets irritated at being rectified by a nerd. "Get lost you 'inflation-bloody-depression'". Thank god, Ranbir knows at least some jargons from the Commerce stream.

Then, with a reminder that he is still on the phone, Ranbir quickly switches gears. "Hey, where are you guys?"

"Canteen"

Ranbir saunters into the canteen, only to be met with the sight of Sushant in full flirt mode with a certain Roma. The hottest girl in the college is sitting next to Sushant and he is trying to decipher the network of lines on her palms. Sushant's pulse rate has already exceeded 75 beats per min, the result of the most beautiful girl in his company.

"Why do you let others take advantage of you being liberal?" Sushant asks, his eyes acting emotional. By the end of this dialogue, he has planted a gentle kiss on Roma's hand.

"You're absolutely right" Roma responds with a sob, her eyes welling up. "Everyone seems to takes advantage of me".

"Take it easy," Sushant pats her hand, "Henceforth, I would shield you from all the evil eyes" and gives a dagger look at the peeping Tom's around.

Sushant notices Ranbir waving out to him from a distance, "Roma, I will give you a buzz in the evening"

Roma gets up to leave. Rain in her eyes. She walks towards the college exit gate.

"*Agar wo mere jaal mei phas gayi hai, to mud kar dekhegi,*" Sushant delivers a Shah rukh style dialogue.

Roma turns around. Sushant wants to shout like a werewolf but makes an emotional face and waves out to her. Almost in slow motion.

"Great going man" Ranbir comments as he approaches Sushant. "*Bhabhi* Material?" he asks, spinning the football in his hand.

"*2 ser doodh ke liye, bakri kaun kharidega?*" Sushant winks.

Raman returns the phone back to Sushant. He has passed without KT's.

"Get cold drinks", Sushant orders. Raman leaves to obey.

Both the besties hug and congratulate each other. "*Bhai-bhai, Bhai-bhai*" they say.

God knows for what reason they say '*Bhai-bhai*'. '*Bhai-bhai*' they said when they wished each other on birthdates. They said '*Bhai-bhai*' when they congratulated each other on achievements (which were few and far between), 'Bhai-bhai' was used as patch up after misunderstanding. Maybe this term gave them a sense of togetherness.

"Let's hit the road," Sushant exclaims spiritedly. The batch-mates listening around could have thought that they had topped the university.

"*Chal gadi nikal*". Sushant orders Raman with the usual authority.

EYES CLASH

The trio cruise along at 120 mph, the norm for the onlookers along the scenic Queens Necklace. All the lovely ladies are greeted with 'I love you'. Careless maneuvering, reflects their carefree attitude. Suddenly, with a screech of tires, they execute a daring U-turn, heading back to their college.

They zoom down the road that lay between the college building and the girls' hostel. Suddenly the brakes are applied. Tyres screech. Documents flutter like confetti. Two gorgeous heads could be seen amidst the whirl of papers. Those were Genelia and Amruta. Both have hidden their face in fright, not knowing how to react to a rocket hurtling towards them at 120 km/hr.

"We're so sorry," Sushant hurriedly apologizes, getting out of the Gypsy. Ranbir follows suit. Raman freezes in his seat.

"What is this, drunken driving?" Genelia's voice rings out in anger, her frustration palpable. "Is this how recklessly you drive?"

This beauty has the adjective of strong to her personality. Her rimless specs with bob cut hair along with the grey blazer that she has worn accentuated her strict disposition. She gives the impression of a rude boss-classy, chic, and beautiful as hell.

She goes to Sushant and questions him. Eye in eye. Sushant is mesmerised by Genelia's hypnotic eyes. He just couldn't take his eyes off her.

"Let it go, Genelia" says a gentler voice attempting to steer Genelia away from Sushant. This is Amruta. An epitome of beauty and politeness. In stark contrast to Genelia, Amruta is timid and petite, averse to creating a scene on the road. She couldn't even bear the stare of the onlookers.

Clad in white salwar kurta, she has worn a simple silver necklace that delicately adorns her neck. The saffron dupatta added a touch of elegance to her ensemble. Her silky brown long hair is glistening like gold in the midday sun. Ranbir stands there like a statue, his gaze fixated on her lips. Dew-kissed, velvet lips. What could he say?

Amruta manages to take Genelia on the other side of the road. They enter the ladies' hostel.

Is this just a fleeting attraction this time, or are they serious? Perhaps, this is not the correct time to jump to conclusions. But, the magnetism of the ladies have pulled these chap well beyond the 'Laxman rekha' of the ladies' hostel. They realise their trespassing only when Jethi, the Nepali lady watch guard, stops them from venturing further.

"*O sahib ji kidhar ko jaata hai, pata nahi hai kya ye ladies hostel hai. Chokra ja nahi sakta hai*" Jethi says in her typical Nepali accent stopping them from venturing into the hostel.

But like sunflowers that follow every moment of the sun, their eyes follow the beauties. Suddenly the sun disappears, and the sunflowers become restless.

"Can I just check in which room she stays?" Ranbir beseeches, unable to contain his curiosity. "Or just tell us the floor and the room number," Sushant adds eagerly.

"Why do you want this information for?" Jethi probes suspiciously.

"Sorry, that is personal", Ranbir says with a naughty smile and winks at Sushant. Sushant reciprocates mischievously.

"Sorry, hum bhi personal information nahi deta hai," Jethi states firmly.

Ranbir takes out a hundred rupee note. "Let us go in."

"*Ek baar bola na nahi*," Jethi stands her ground.

"*Ajeeb hai, kalyug ka zamana hi nahi raha*," Sushant says, frowning.

Jethi is in no mood to relent. She pushes them.

"*Are dhakka kisko deti hai be. Hat mat laga. Aurat hai isliye kadar kar rahe hai varna*," says Sushant .

The noise decibel had made the dean of the hostel come out. She is a big fat lady, just like most of the Opera Singers.

"*Varna Kya, ha ???*" the stern voice of Miss Vaswani roars. She stares intensely through her mammoth specks. Miss Vaswani has developed aversion towards male species. She is an Androphobic. A total male hater. The scandals, the rape incidents have asserted her belief that 'All men are dogs'. This is the reason why even the watchman was a woman.

Gone with the Wind are the fighters.

When the boys get back into the Gypsy van they see a form lying on the rear seat with Amruta's photo on it. Ranbir's eyes sparkle. He takes it as a signal from heaven. He looks at Sushant and says, "God wants us to meet. *Lagta hai, Rab ne bana di Jodi*".

JUST FOR A GLIMPSE!

Every year, the college celebrates Dahi Handi, a tradition involving the formation of a human pyramid to break an earthen pot suspended thirty feet in the air by a rope. This time the event is organised on the road opposite the girls' hostel. This gives an official license to the boys to hang out in front of the girl's hostel. Naturally, it is the Dean's worst nightmare.

Ranbir has learnt a few peacock dance steps from Sushant. But dancing was never Ranbir's forte. Ranbir joines the banjo crew, parading in front of the girls' hostel. The mood is euphoric, and soon the pulsating music rules over Ranbir's senses. He dances his Ganpati Visarjan dance. His dance elicits more laughter than claps. Sushant misses this as he had gone to his relative a day before for Janmashtami pooja and is supposed to return late evening.

Ranbir is hopeful that he might get to see Amruta, if she comes to girl hostel's balcony. The view of the balcony is partially obscured by tree branches. Ranbir organises his team to form a human pyramid. Amongst the roaring crowd, Ranbir ascends the top of human tower. He scans for the face amid the onlookers from the girl's hostel. As luck would have it, Amruta emerges onto the balcony, oblivious to the fact that somebody is willing to give his right arm, just to get a glimpse of her.

Ranbir is so captivated by her appearance that he forgets to break the pot. The pyramid couldn't hold itself.

He gets off-balanced, and the pyramid collapses. The rest of his day is spent at home nursing his swollen hips.

In the evening, Sushant hurries up to the terrace, finding Ranbir seated at the outer edge of the terrace, their customary sitting spot but this time with a cushion under his rump. This is their daily meeting point in the evening during sunset.

The sky resembles an enormous orange Imax dome screen. The waves crashing against the tetrapods could give the Dolby system a run for its money. The air has conditioned itself, with a pleasant temperature of 26 degrees Celcius. Almost a Romantic Movie-watching experience.

This was the place where all the topics ranging from the latest crush to the newest apps were discussed.

"Why are you sitting like this?" Sushant asks Ranbir, watching his uncomfortable side-to-side moments.

"Ladki ki chakkar ne suja di." says Ranbir keeping his hands on his bums. Sushant tries to control his laughter.

"Wish she was with me at this moment," Ranbir sighs, watching the sun take a dip in the water. "It's just impossible to take my mind off that innocent face"

"I am in the same boat. Those eyes are haunting me, "Sushant confesses, his voice trailing into a distant state of reverie.

They both let the silence envelop them, watching the fleeting clouds perform drama on the canvas before them. The hue and the colours are the colours of hope. As the twilight descends, the neon Signs begin to flicker at a distance. Queen's necklace begins to glitter with the headlights of the passing vehicles.

Ranbir hears a voice calling him. It is his mother's. She needs him to run an errand for her. It's truly irksome when small tasks intrude upon romantic moments, disrupting the flow of tender moments.

"Unwanted Interval." Ranbir mutters in irritation, his mood interrupted by the errand.

"Hey, I will come down too," Sushant chimes in. "My parents have gone to our native place; I've got to take dinner parcel for Sanjana and myself."

"I'll get home-made food for you. Why spend on hotel food?" Ranbir offers.

"*Are kyu aunty ko taklif*?" Sushant retorts.

"Not at all. Mom will start the preparations only after I bring the wheat flour. You know how moms love to showcase their culinary skills,"

Ranbir winks.

"Alright then,"Sushant grins.

"And what's this 'Taklif Waklif thing?" Ranbir asks, playfully punching Sushant on his shoulder

"O.K, boss '*Bhai-bhai*'," Sushant garlands his left hand on Ranbir's nape of the neck and pulls him down. Ranbir pushes him back. Bruce Lee's spirit seems to possess them as they hit each other playfully while climbing down the stairs.

After getting the tiffins for three, Ranbir enters Sushant's house. Sushant's 12-year-old younger sister, Sanjana, opens the door.

"Hi Sanju, What's up?" greets Ranbir.

"Getting bored alone bhayya, was on Facebook," Sanjana replies.

Ranbir hands over tiffin to her. Sushant instructs her to lay the table for three.

"OK. Let me log off my account," saying this, Sanjana heads towards the laptop.

"Wait, don't log off!," Ranbir suddenly exclaims as though struck by a brilliant idea. "Sanjana, wait, I will be back in a while." Saying this, Ranbir rushes out of the room and returns with Amruta's bio-data that he collected from the Gypsy Van.

"Type AMRUTA SAHASTRABUDDHE, in the search column," Ranbir instructs, peering into the resume.

Sanjana is a sweet obedient girl. Without any further questions, she types the words in the search column. The list displays at least twelve 'Amruta Sahastrabuddhes'.

"Yes, send her Friend's request," Sushant excitedly urges Sanjana, pointing to the one donning a pink salwar kurta.

Sanjana sends the request and logs off the laptop to have their food.

Sushant lays the plate for the three. Sanjani sits on one end of the table, while Ranbir occupies the other end. Sushant sits in the middle serving food. Ranbir through a sign language communicates something to Sushant, and Sushant reciprocates.

"Dada, when will you teach me this sign language?", Sanjana pleads with a giggle.

"Hey, this is boys' secret code language, not meant for children", winks Sushant.

Ranbir hi-fives him with his left hand, chomping on the aloo-gobi dressed in chapatti. Ranbir's mother had parcelled Steamed rice, dal fry, aloo gobi, chappatis, aam ka achar and papad. Ranbir had been instructed to return later for a serving of Aam ras, a thick liquid mango puree, as it was decided at the last moment and needed some time to get ready.

As soon as they finish their dinner, Ranbir goes to the laptop and asks Sanjana to check her account.

"Hurray!!! The friend request is accepted," shouts Ranbir. '*Bhai-bhai, bhai-bhai*'. No chance that he would think of Aam Ras now.

Excitedly, Ranbir scrolls Amruta's account. He navigates to the 'about' button. Her status says 'single'. She is a first-year SCIENCE student. Her native place – Karnataka. Her 'interested in' column was not filled. Her most recent status update – Visiting Mahalaxmi Mandir at 10.00 a.m. tomorrow. The use of full spelling indicates Amruta is still not in the 'Yo' culture.

The Bus

Ranbir couldn't afford to miss this opportunity to meet Amruta. He reaches the bus stop opposite girls' hostel at 9.45 a.m., a bit early to ensure he wouldn't miss her arrival. At exactly 10.00 a.m., Amruta shows up. The bus arrives and they board the same bus. Amruta heads towards the ladies' seat. Ranbir takes a seat behind her. Ranbir purchases a ticket to Mahalaxmi Temple.

Amruta hands a 500 Rs. note. The conductor gets irked at the sight of a bapu note.

"*Aho madam, sutte dya*," the conductor snaps, which roughly translates to "Hey madam, give exact change."

"I am sorry, I don't have change," Amruta apologizes.

The Mumbai conductors are perpetually irritated with the commuters not dispensing exact change. He loses his cool. "Why do you travel in bus, take the taxi instead?" the conductor says almost fuming. "Are you travelling for the first time?"

This is Ranbir's chance to intervene. Amruta is thoroughly embarrassed by the conductor's attitude.

"Get down at the next stop", the conductor warns.

"Excuse me," Ranbir intervenes.

Amruta looks at Ranbir.

"*Aap se nahi, in se baat kar raha hu*," Ranbir says swaying his glance from Amruta towards the conductor.

Ranbir speaks in Marathi, "*He paha, tya Mumbai madhe navin aahet. Aaplya pahunya aahet. Atithi devo bhava, hi aapli sanskriti aahe. Mala sanga kiti paise zhalet te?* (She is new in Mumbai. Guests are treated as God in our culture. You shouldn't treat her like this. Tell me how much is the fare?)

"Fifteen rupees," the conductor replies.

Ranbir hands out the exact change.

Amruta is relieved to have the ordeal over. Her face is crimson with embarrassment. "Thank you."

"My pleasure," reciprocates Ranbir, later thinking if 'No mention' was more appropriate at that time.

Mahalaxmi stop arrives and Ranbir alights first. He goes southwards and turns back to check out Amruta.

Amruta has walked in the opposite direction.

Ranbir finds himself uttering Sushant-style dialogues, "*Agar Rab ne hamari Jodi banai hai, to woh mud ke dekhegi.*" At that moment she turns around. Ranbir is taken by surprise, He has crazily hoped for her to turn but didn't expect that she would. He is further awestruck when she waves at him. Sushant doesn't move from his place. He actually thinks it's surreal about what has happened.

Amruta walks towards him, "Hello, thanks again for the help. You spoke to the conductor in Marathi and used the word '*Navin*' which means 'new,' right?"

"Yes, I told him that you were new here," Ranbir replies.

"Hmmm, I kind of figured it out," Amruta says, "How do you know that I am new here?"

"After the van incident, I saw you going inside Girl's hostel," Ranbir says toungue in cheek.

"Was that you in the van? I don't recall seeing you."

"Good that you didn't see me," Ranbir chuckles.

Amruta smiles. Ranbir feels at ease.

"Do you know Central Canteen in the J.J. College campus?"

"Yes," Ranbir replies, curious about where this is leading to.

Can we meet tomorrow in canteen, at 11 a.m.?" she asks.

Were the words true!!! he couldn't believe what is being said to him. He just nodds his head. Actually he wants to let out a scream of joy!

At a book store owned by Raman's father, in his absence, Sushant is killing his time in the afternoon, sprawling on the chair outside the shop. Raman, on the other hand, Raman is standing inside the shop, leaning against the cash counter. He is handling the store in his father's absence.

"Hey, look, that girl is coming this way," Sushant alerts Raman. "Don't give her whatever she asks for," he says hastily, leaping over the counter and hiding himself beneath it.

"Papa ko pata chala to chillaenge" Raman makes a sad face. "Laxmi ati hai tab mana nahi karna chahiye."

"Aur agar tumne kitab di to mai itna chillaounga, ke zindagi bhar kan mei ungli dale hue phirega".

"Excuse me, may I have DR. Steven's book on Chemical Reactions," Genelia orders the book, her eyes run through the piles of book.

The book she sought is prominently displayed on the front shelf. Raman quickly positions himself in front of it, blocking her view.

"Sorry Madam, due to great demand, we are currently out of stock. We have already placed an order and the delivery is expected in a few days."

"Can you recommend any other book store where I can get it today? It's urgent. If I purchase online, it will take a few days to get delivered." Genelia pleads. Raman panics at the thought of losing out a customer.

"Ok., O.k wait. let me check nowww........Noooooo," Raman whines in pain as Sushant grabs him below the belt.

"Madam, please come within the next two days, I will make sure to arrange the book for you," Raman said, forcing a smiling face in the moments of pain.

"Sorry, can't wait so long. I will manage from some other book-store". Genelia says disappointed.

"Mam, you will find these kinds of books in the Fort Area. You can try out there".

"O.K. Thanks, I will try."

Genelia turns and climbs down the stairs. And when she has gone a little further a voice calls her from behind.

"Excuse me, Hi I am Sushant, You might have heard my name," says the filmy buff.

Genelia quips, "I might not have heard your name, but I'm sure I've seen your face," recalling the speeding van incident she says, "Aren't you the guy from that day?"

Sushant gets thrown off a bit. "Sorry again for that. Actually, that day we had passed our exams."

"But you must be careful on road, it's risky driving like that, not only for others but also for your life".

"I will keep that in mind the next time I pass," jokes Sushant to lighten the mood. "By the way, I'm a science student and I have the book that you require, I overheard your conversation with the book store owner. If you can meet me here tomorrow at 6.00, I will be able to give you the book."

Genelia gets excited "Oh! Thank you so much. I need that book. But wouldn't you need it yourself?"

"No no.. those are my last year's books" Sushant lies.

Sushant is fascinated by Genelia. He could have resorted to any means to talk to her.

"Let me know when and where I can collect the book", Genelia says, and then she does the unexpected, she extended her hand, " Hi, I am Genelia Bangera, ?"

Ranbir shakes her hand and, involuntary, touches his heart. Genelia shares her cell number.

Had the stars changed their course? Had the world entered into a bliss mode? The setting sun appeared heart-shaped today. Interlacing of mango, pink and blue shades in the sky, added to the romantic feel. From the vantage point of terrace, they could see, tiny people moving along the queen's necklace promenade. But today couples seemed to outnumber the lone populace.

That night both of our lovestruck boys couldn't go to sleep. They were just delirious with the thought of meeting the girls. That night they eagerly waited for the sunrise in their life.

First Heartache

A dashing-looking Ranbir enters the Central Canteen, 20 minutes late. He has left no stone unturned to look his best. His perfume could be smelled from a distance of 2 km. In the informally dressed students around, his blazer made him stand apart.

Amruta, punctual to the minute, is already seated on the chair, dressed in a white salwar with an orange dupatta. She waves out to Ranbir.

"O.k. so, I have already wasted 20 minutes, don't want to delay it any further," declares Ranbir and takes out a red rose from his shirt pocket "I love you."

Amruta is dumbfounded with this unexpected gesture. "Excuse me, what is this?" she asks, her voice tinged with hesitation.

"A Proposal, why not?", Ranbir responds, confused with Amruta's reactions.

Amruta glances around nervously. "Are you serious?"

"Of course," Ranbir affirmed, "You invited me here on a date, right? And I like you, so why waste time?"

Amruta notices the people around staring at the red rose, their curiosity aroused. She suddenly stands up to leave.

"Listen, Ranbir, this is quite embarrassing for me. You are mistaken. I asked you here to return the change that I owe to you."

"What!" Ranbir's panic is evident, "Was that the only reason you asked me here".

"I couldn't bear the weight of a favour from a stranger, so I had to return the money. Look, I am finding this all very embarrassing, I have to leave", saying this Amruta hurriedly leaves the canteen.

Ranbir is devasted. He is not prepared for such turn of events. He is madly in love with her. He remains in his seat stunned. Amruta disappears from his sight.

The sky over Marine Lines is cloudy. Traffic is a mess. It has drizzled unexpectedly and the promenade is deserted. The rain has taken everybody by surprise. This rain is due to a 'Western disturbance' not the most awaited 'Monsoon rains' Ranbir is seated in his place on the terrace, but this time with a cigarette.

Sushant is baffled at this behaviour and asks him the reason for smoking.

Ranbir, for the first time in his life, is not able to express himself.

Sushant looks into his eyes "You don't look alright." Ranbir's eyes are gleaming.

Ranbir suddenly breaks down in Sushant's arms.

"I think, I can't live without her," he sobs. "She said that she is embarrassed and walked away".

"Tell me exactly, what has happened?" Sushant, concerned, probes further.

Ranbir recounts his story.

"Shit! You proposed to her immediately? Are yaar, what was the hurry?" Sushant rebukes. "You gave her an impression that you were desperate. You should have taken it slow, gone on more dates, and spent time together. You should have made her feel comfortable, taken time to understand her; known her likes-dislikes".

"Shit, shit, shit", Ranbir curses himself "Could I just rewind the time? Not propose to her, at least spend some more time with her at the table," Ranbir laments. Sushant throws away the cigarette from his hand.

"If *Rab ne bana di hai Jodi*, then you would meet again." Sushant tries to cheer him up, but Ranbir's face stays passive.

"C'mon, assist me in the dance rehearsals for the Rose day. Got to impress Genelia," Sushant wants Ranbir to stay busy and come out of the depression.

SECOND HEARTACHE

Commerce lectures get over. It is time for science students to enter the campus. So the corridors of Elphinstone college are usually crowded at this point of time. Sushant's eyes fall on Genelia. She is dressed in white apron and is walking towards the laboratory. She has obtained special permission from college authorities to use the laboratory for her experiments.

Sushant wades his way towards her and intentionally bumps into her, "Hi, quite early today I suppose".

"Yes, I joined the college quite late. I have to complete some experiment assignments."

"Hey I have the book with me, can I give it to you now, it's quite heavy?"

"*Neki aur pooch pooch*, I am dying to lay my hands on it."

Sushant hands over the book.

"I can't thank you enough", Genelia flips through the book. 'Hey! You can join me in the lab. Actually, you could be of help", says an excited Genelia, glad to have assistance at hand.

Sushant is in a fix. What would a Commerce student know anything about those experiments? But he couldn't have afforded to miss a chance to be in Genelia's company, so he decides to accompany her.

The smelly Lab makes Sushant dizzy, but his love smells better. Soon, they go near a table whereon a lot of apparatus are kept.

Genelia instructs Sushant to pass the flask. Not knowing, how a flask looks, Sushant passes her a Test Tube.

"I said flask, flask", Genelia parts her hands to the size of a flask.

It had only been 4 years of matriculation, but in these years, Sushant has forgotten how a flask looks like. To avoid being caught, he just looks into his mobile and appears busy. Genelia goes and collects the flask herself. Soon she starts mixing various chemicals in the test tubes.

"Is this some new experiment?" Sushant asks.

"Don't you know this one?" Genelia asks perplexed.

"It's been a year now," Sushant gives the excuse.

Genelia starts mixing chemicals one after another. Sushant keenly observes her.

"Pass me ammonium chloride please", Genelia requests picking up a beaker. Sushant's face turns pale. He panics. But, he has to respond. Acting busy on mobile he picks up a bottle containing a yellow powder and hands over to Genelia. The powder passed is TNT.

"*Terrorist ho kya, blast karna hai?*" Genelia laughs, assuming it as a prank from Sushant.

"Blast?" Sushant is startled.

Aren't you aware that even if you add 10 grams of TNT in Hcl it would create a blast enough to bring this laboratory down.

"*Chemical locha ho jata...yaarr?,*" laughs Sushant trying to keep a brave face and then scared as hell keeps looking at the yellow powder that he has just passed.

After completion, they head to a nearby Cafe Coffee Day. It is almost vacant. Finding a nice corner seat, they order two cups of coffee, they settle in the relaxed atmosphere.

"Genelia V Shetty," reads out Sushant, from the book placed on the coffee table. "So you are from Tamil Nadu, right?"

"NO Karnataka," Genelia corrects with a frown on her face as though a racial comment is passed.

"Why the frown? You are a South Indian. It doesn't make a difference to me, be it Tamil Nadu or Kerala." Sushant responds, trying to play it off lightly.

"Most of the people here assume that all South Indians speak the same language. But our culture, work ethic, language differ a lot. And it matters a lot to me." Genelia says coming in her elements.

"Cool it, man, look at yourself . You are almost fuming. Ok. I am sorry it is Kerala, right?", Sushant couldn't control his laughter.

'No Karnataka," says Genelia playfully hitting the book on his head.

The two seem to be getting closer and enjoying each other's company. Soon the hot coffee is served.

"Do you live with your parents in Kerrrrr..... sorry Karnataka," Sushant chides her, sipping on the coffee.

Genelia's expression shift, and she looked a bit uncomfortable. She places the coffee cup back on the table.

"Hey, I'm sorry, I won't say Kerala again," Sushant assures her, not wanting a second blow from the book.

"You are my friend now, so I must share the truth, right?" says Genelia, talking to herself more than with Sushant.

"Of course how could true friendship happen if it is based on lies?" Sushant agrees.

"Ok, the truth is, I come from a broken family. My parents are divorced", Genelia reveals with a hint of bitterness.

"I am sorry", Sushant expresses his empathy.

"I never thought that I'd be discussing about my family with anyone. I don't know why I revealed it to you. I think I consider you as a very close friend of mine.", says Genelia. For Sushant, it is a totally different sight to see a lady with strict disposition get so very emotional.

"With whom do you stay?" Sushant asks, showing concern.

"As per the court's order, I am staying with my mother in Kerala", Genelia says.

"Kerala !!!", Sushant exclaims, almost spilling out some coffee.

"Oops, Karnataka", she covers her face in embarrassment. "See what you have done", Genelia throws a tissue paper at Sushant. Suddenly they break into a fit of laughter.

"Thank god you smiled, I thought this coffee session was going to end on a really cold note," Sushant smiles.

"Friends should always be told the truth. You asked me about my parents, so I told you the facts but henceforth don't discuss them with me," Genelia says, looking away.

Sushant notices the hurt in her eyes. "I understand."

"I get turned off by liars and hypocrites," Genelia says fiddling with the coffee mug.

"Drink your coffee fast, lest it turns into cold coffee. I would have to pay more," Sushant jokes, but deep down a panic chord has struck.

THE ROSE DAY

It's Rose Day. Two Dance groups have made it to final and are on the stage for the faceoff. Sushant's group is representing commerce side. The second group is from Science stream. The students from both the faculties have come to support their respective dance group. The atmosphere is pulsating. Flood lights, lasers, and all the other gizmos give a concert like feel to the event. Tension and the excitement could be felt in the air.

The announcer introduces the science team first. The crowd receives them with a deafening roar. The leader from the science stream attacks the dance floor first with a head spin. He has metals pierced in his eyebrows, tongue and ears, which create a halo effect when he spins continuously. It is amazing to see a science student perform a feat like that. The onlookers cheer him.

The referee introduces the Commerce side. Now it is Sushant's time to perform. Sushant walks briskly at the centre of the stage and suddenly enters into a slow-motion mode. It is a spectacle to behold. It looks as though some kind of live special effect is playing before the eyes. The crowd is awestruck. The crowd swings Sushant's side. His name echoes in the air.

Both the groups present their dancing skills. It is but obvious who the winner would be. The leader of the opposite team plays foul by pushing Sushant. Sushant loses his balance and falls on the stage. Sushant's group retaliate.

The referee intervenes, and soon the situation is brought under control.

Both the groups perform as though their life depends on it. But in Sushants case, much more is on stake. He knows that Genelia would come to know of the truth of his being a Commerce Student as he represents the the Commerce side. So he just wants to impress Genelia with his dancing skills. He expects his talent to make up for his lie.

Sushant has given a performance of a life time. The spectators have just one word for him. "Cyclone – The one that sweeps everybody off their feet." The spectators are enthralled.

It's result time. The air is filled with the support for Sushant. Both the groups' members are looking expectantly at the trophy but Sushant is searching for Genelia in the crowd.

Sushant's group is declared the winner. Sushant is flocked by the spectators, but even in this din, he manages to locate Genelia. Sushant wades his way towards Genelia.

"How was the performance?" Sushant asks.

"You are a great performer both on stage and also in real life. You lie as effortlessly as you dance." says Genelia, with disgust.

Sushant knows that trouble is brewing for him.

"Please don't misunderstand me. I had no other way to make friends with you", Sushant says in a pleading tone.

"If friendship had to happen, it would have happened anyways" Genelia is furious." But you chose a lie to start a relationship. How can I trust you henceforth?"

"Please, for God's sake, try to understand me", Sushant pleads. He understands Genelia's body language. Genelia has turned sideways, obviously meaning she wants to go away.

"My parents had warned me against people like you. They were right. Anyway, thanks for the book and yes, it was a very good performance. Good bye," with that, Genelia walks away.

Sushant knows he is at fault. He just watches her go. Soon he finds himself alone in the crowd.

The queen's necklace is glittering as usual, but smoke from two cigarettes has made the view from the terrace a little hazy. Sushant has realized the pain and anguish felt by Ranbir.

The questions like "What next?", "How would we make them understand?", "Is this the end?" haunts them both.

"She doesn't understand; how much I like her. Would I never be able to meet her again?", Ranbir's voice is filled with a sense of longing as he stares at the dark expanse of the sky above the Queen's Necklace.

"She called me a liar," Sushant sighs, his voice tinged with depression. "But really, was there any other way to even get her attention?"

Both of these young men had experienced relationships before. In the era of Facebook, WhatsApp and various social media platforms, it is easy to engage in flirtations. However, those past experiences paled in comparison to what they were feeling now – a deep and genuine love. Now we could say for sure – OUR BOYS WERE IN TRUE LOVE.

The pain of their love not being with them is overwhelming. The couples on the Marine Dive, who have turned their back on the world, cuddling each other, not caring for the world, only intensify their longing. They could relate to every lyric of Arijit Singh's songs on heartbreaks, as if those songs were written specifically for them.

They decide to get over their depression. They delete all the songs from their mobile. They try not to think of them. But, some way or the other their thoughts came and then it became unbearable. Depression seemed to have become their constant companion.

They couldn't take it anymore. They couldn't bear their absence. No matter what they did, they couldn't stop thinking about them.

"We have to meet them and convince them. Maybe that time was not right. Maybe we were too hasty in our approach. Maybe they could have a change of heart if we speak to them again." analysed Ranbir.

"You are right, we have to meet them", Sushant says, exhaling the last puff.

The sun rises with a new hope. Ranbir loiters around the bus stop for the whole day; in the expectation of meeting Amruta or at least getting a glimpse of her. His efforts are in vain. There is no way of knowing her whereabouts. He calls up Sanjana to check if Amruta has made any status updates.

"No bhaiyya, no recent updates," Sanjana says, surfing on Amruta's FB account. Ranbir just doesn't know what to do. He is engulfed in a sense of despair.

Sushant is desperate to meet Genelia too. He searches for Genelia in the college and sees her hanging out with the B'boying group. Not caring about the strained relation, Sushant goes straight to them.

"Excuse me, can I speak to you for a moment?" Sushant asks, his voice tinged with sincerity.

"Genelia, is everything fine?", confirms the metal-pierced leader of the b'boying group, flexing his tattooed arm.

"Yeah, it's ok," saying this Genelia excuses herself from the group. She approaches Sushant.

"I am Sorry to have lied. I did whatever came to my mind at that time. Hell, I feel awful!" Sushant says in remorse.

"It is so typical of you boys. You carry the word 'sorry' in your pocket like a Card. Swipe it and you are done, right?.", Genelia fires.

"I wouldn't even have had the opportunity of speaking to you if I hadn't lied to you. The fact is I love you from the bottom of my heart", Sushant's voice chokes.

Genelia rolls her eyes, "Do you even know the meaning of love? It's not something you say to every other girl that you know.

"I might have flirted with many, but that was not love for sure. See, I am having difficulty in breathing now. I am breaking just at the thought of you not being a part of my life.", Sushant's eyes well up.

"O.K. so now you are talking about life. Let's keep aside love aside for a moment; do you even know what life is?", Genelia asks. "You don't even know where your career is heading to. I am sure you wouldn't have an answer if I asked you 'Where do you see yourself ten years from now?'

"What has love to do with career?", Sushant retaliates.

"There you are – impractical, Filmy. What are you pursuing, Commerce? Tell me what are your future plans? Genelia challenges.

"Simple. I will get a job after college."

"What kind of job"

"Any job that a person gets after college"

See, there you are. Without focus without ambition. Get real before it's too late. We girls are much more practical. I would not like to talk more about this. Just introspect. If you are mature enough you will find the answers yourself."

"Oh so there you are, a typical Careerist. How would you understand what true love is? Have you caught any rich fish in your net?", says Sushant almost fuming. Genelia looks at him aghast.

"Girls are disloyal gold diggers," continues Sushant. "We boys love truly and can do anything for true love".

Taken aback by the harsh words, Genelia says "Ok, you say you can do anything, alright. Meet me at the J.J Hospital morgue at 11 tonight. Prove your love," in a fit of anger, Genelia stomps away.

MISUNDERSTANDING AT MORGUE.

'J.J. Hospital *Murdaghar*', the huge banner looks eerie in the sole yellow dim light of the street outside the Morgue. Genelia is standing at the entrance, surfing her mobile. Sushant is taken aback at her courage of standing alone in that spooky looking deserted place.

"How long have you been waiting here? Sushant asks concerned.

"Just came a few seconds ago" was an indifferent reply. Her icy tone leaves Sushant on a guilt trip , unsure of how to bridge the gap between them. He just stands, eyes downcast.

"Here take this", Genelia hands over Dairy milk chocolate. Sushant is flummoxed at this.

"Don't have wrong ideas." Genelia clarifies, "You have to force open the mouth of at least 3 dead bodies and put this chocolate inside. If you can do this, maybe then I'll believe you're willing to do anything for me".

A chill went down Sushant's spine at the thought of entering the morgue alone at night. But he has to prove his love. How could he back down? He accepts the challenge. He takes the chocolate and enters the morgue.

The door opens with a creaking sound. Inside the air is chilled and foggy, the result of 0' degree of temperature maintained to preserve the dead. The pungent smell makes Sushant want to puke. He holds his hand on his nose as he moved towards the drawers containing the bodies. He put his hand on a handle to pull the drawer. The drawer opens with a screeching sound. It has an old man's mutilated body who had recently met with an accident. Stitches on his forehead are a gory sight. Sushant feeds the chocolate in his mouth.

Feeding the corpse, he runs at a rusty basin besides the entry door and vomits.

The task is not completed yet. Returning back to the adjacent drawer he tucks at the handle. But the drawer refuses to budge. Sushant applies force to pull the drawer. This time the drawer opens revealing a body of a young man. Blood could be seen trickling down his face.

When Sushant tries to open his mouth to put the Cadbury, the boy opens the mouth himself and bites Sushant's finger.

The incident shakes the daylights out of Sushant.

Out of nowhere, two more boys emerge out from the hiding. One of them, is the leader of the b-boying group, the one with metals dangling from his face. The other his assistant. The two punch Sushant in the stomach. Sushant collapses on the floor. Sushant is held porcine on the floor by the three.

"You think you are a hero, ha?", sneers the boy, who had come out of the drawer, holding Sushant's neck.

"With fractured bones do you think you can dance anymore?", taunts the leader.

"Yes, I will", saying this Sushant manages to turn and hit him in his groin. In pain, the boy steps backwards. Sushant takes this opportunity and frees himself from the clutches of the two other boys. One of the boy has tomato sauce smeared on his face. Sushant catches him first and punches him on his face, causing a gash near his eye.

"Now, this looks genuine blood, bloody bastard" saying this Sushant gives him an uppercut.

The scuffle between them creates a noise loud enough to alert the hospital staff. Suddenly 6-7 ward boys enter the room and catch all the boys.

"What an amazing place to fight", comments an elderly ward boy.

"*Are murdo ko to chain se rehne do*", adds another.

They are caught and presented before the head matron in the casualty ward.

"Sister, don't call the police. These three will land into trouble.", Sushant implores.

"Sister, we had just come to scare him", says the boy wiping off the tomato ketchup.

The Matron is an elderly kind nurse. She looks at all the boys carefully.

"You look from a good family," she says.

"*Kya hua ladki ka mamla hai*', chides one ward boy tearing a Gutka pouch.

Sushant looks daggers at him. The ward boy freezes in his place.

"I don't want to see you boys in lock up. Don't get physical. I am leaving you this time with a warning", says the matron.

The three hold their heads down.

Sushant along with the other three walks out of the morgue. Genelia is at the gate unaware of the happening of the events inside. She is surprised to see all of them walking out together. She had expected to see Sushant running on his heels.

Sushant doesn't utter a word to her. His eyes are red with anger and hatred. He now views Genelia as a girl who tried to harm him. He couldn't believe that a person that he loved so much would do such an act. He is totally hurt.

"Sushant you are bleeding", Genelia's eyes are saucers, when she watches blood trickling down his lips.

"Shut up, don't act", saying this Sushant just walks away.

"Hey guys, what did you do to him? I just told you to scare him away and you took this opportunity to settle your personal rivalry...shame on you guys."

THE INSULT

Raman's father, Mr. Varma, is back from his tour. He is a stern man who takes great pride in his bookstore. One evening, as he is going through his monthly stock tally, he notices a science book missing from the shelves. His brows furrow in concern as he double-checks the records, confirming that the book has indeed been taken by a certain customer.

He calls his son. Raman, into his study where he manages the book store's accounts and operations. "Raman, have you noticed the missing science book from the inventory?" Mr. Varma's tone is firm, signalling that he means business.

"Missing book? I haven't noticed", Raman gulps a lump in his throat.

Mr. Varma's eyes narrow as he studies his son's face.

Raman hesitates, a guilty expression crossing his features. "Sushant took it"

"He is studying with you, right? Why does he need a Science book?"

"It's for a reason", Raman chokes

Mr. Varma's patience are running thin. "And what reason did he give you?"

Raman's voice is soft, almost apologetic. "He said he wanted to gift it to a girl he liked."

Mr. Varma's eyes harden. "So, he's using my book store as a library to impress a girl?"

"I guess so, Dad."

Mr. Varma is now visibly furious. "Call Sushant. He needs to come here and make the payment immediately."

Raman nods, his fingers trembling slightly as he dials Sushant's number. He holds the phone to his ears, his heart pounding, while his father's stern presence looms nearby.

As the call connected, Raman takes a deep breath. "Sushant, Raman here. Can you come to the bookstore, please?"

A few minutes later, a chime of the door announces Sushant's arrival. His face is slightly apprehensive when he notices Raman's father standing nearby.

"Hello, Raman. You called?"

Raman cleared his throat, feeling the weight of the situation. "Yes, Sushant. We need to talk."

His father steps forward, his voice stern as he addresses Sushant. "Do you remember taking "The Science book?"

"Yes, sir."

"Have you made the payment for it?" Raman's father's voice is staunch.

"Sir," Sushant says, his voice apologetic, "I apologize for not making the payment for the book. But, if it's possible, I could make the payment in the next month. I'm going through a bit of a crunch right now."

Raman's father's stern expression remains unchanged, and his eyes narrow as he listens to Sushant's plea. Sushant can feel the intensity of his gaze, and it makes him uneasy.

"A crunch, you say?" Raman's father's voice is laced with scepticism, his tone dripping with sarcasm. "I'm glad to see that a crunch in your pocket hasn't stopped you from taking books without paying."

Sushant's cheeks flush with embarrassment. He knows he is at fault, but he hadn't expected Raman's father to be so unrelenting. He takes a deep breath, his fingers involuntarily clenching into fists.

"Sir, I genuinely intend to pay for the book," Sushant persists "I am just asking for a little time, until next month."

Raman's father's lips curl into a disdainful smirk. "Ah, next month, you say? How convenient. Do you think we run a charity here? Are you under the impression that we can just let things slide because you have a crunch? I have noticed you sprawl in our car. Command Raman at will. Who do you think you are?

Sushant's heart sinks as he feels the weight of the insult. He hadn't expected Raman's father to be so callous and dismissive. He could feel his pride and self-esteem crumbling under the weight of the situation.

"But of course, how could I forget?" Raman's father's voice dripped with sarcasm. "You're the son of a martyr, aren't you? How dare I forget to consider that while running a business? It's not like you're the only one dealing with financial issues."

Sushant's fists clench tighter, his nails digging into his palms. He is now struggling to keep his composure, feeling a mix of anger and humiliation. He looks up, meeting Raman's father's gaze.

"I'll make the payment right now," Sushant says in a firm voice, his pride wounded.

Sushant's initial feelings of shame and regret began to morph into something else – anger. The sting of Raman's father's insults and disregard for his family's sacrifice fuelled a fire within him. He couldn't believe that someone who knew his background would treat him with such callousness.

Raman's father raises an eyebrow, seemingly taken aback by Sushant's sudden shift in demeanour. "I will arrange the money and bring it to you before the day ends."

Without waiting for any further response, Sushant turns on his heel and walks away, his heart pounding in his chest. He is angry, hurt and humiliated.

Sushant's heart sinks as he watches his mother count the few crumpled notes in her hand. Her brow is furrowed with worry, and he could see the lines of exhaustion etched on her face. She had been working tirelessly to make ends meet since his father's sacrifice, and the burden of their financial struggles weighed heavily on her.

Sushant looks away, his emotions a tangled mess. He couldn't help feeling disappointed and frustrated.

A borrowed book, a simple science book that holds a price tag of a few hundred rupees – a sum that was expensive if not unaffordable for Sushant's modest financial circumstances.

He slams the money on the counter of the bookstore and leaves.

A PHOTO FROM THE PAST.

Sushant gazes at the old photograph of his father in his military uniform, his chest adorned with medals that symbolise his bravery and honour. But behind the veil of valour, Sushant carries the weight of an untold story that shattered his family.

Sushant's father, Major Mohan Rane, was an esteemed officer in the Indian military. He had always been a beacon of courage and integrity, instilling these values in his son from an early age. However, fate had a cruel twist in store for their family.

In a mall, Major Mohan Rane stood before the intricate web of wires and mechanisms that made up the bomb. He knew that the stakes were high; the device had to be carefully deconstructed to prevent a catastrophe.

Vikram's companion, Lieutenant Roy, stood by his side. The responsibility weighed heavily on both of them as they prepared to dismantle the bomb.

Now came a point where a decision to cut between a green and a red wire had to be made. Roy suggested cutting off the green wire, while Mohan insisted on red. Roy said that he had insider's tip with regards to that particular bomb and vouched for the accuracy of his information.

With a deep breath, Vikram cut the wire that Roy suggested. The onlookers waited for a sign that the bomb had been defused. Instead, a chilling click followed by a series of beeps filled the mall, signalling impending disaster. People panicked. Started running helter-skelter leading to stampede.

The blast caused destruction, and lives were lost. News outlets picked up the story, portraying Major Mohan Rane as the person responsible for the explosion. The media questioned his competence, labelling him as the one who failed to prevent the tragedy and the weight of the accusation was suffocating.

As days turned into weeks, Mohan's anguish deepened. His friends and relatives kept distance from him. Mohan's spirit was shattered. He struggled to find solace in a world that had turned against him. A heart attack made him rest in peace.

A CHANGED ATTITUDE

A film shoot is scheduled on the Marine lines flyover bridge so the traffic is diverted. People are not allowed on the promenade. The place wears a deserted look.

"These celebrities are just lucky. They get paid for looking good. Just by-heart some lines and deliver the dialogues, that's it", Sushant's voice has a tone of disgust

"Don't be under the wrong impression, Sushant. Shooting is not a child's play. Even actors have to work their arse out." Ranbir says reading Sushant's agitated face.

"But they get paid in lakhs and crores", Sushant protests.

"Who has stopped you from earning then?", Ranbir says. "Just look at ourselves. What are we doing with life? We don't even care when we flunk in exams. Where are we heading to?" Ranbir speaks passionately.

"Isn't love everything in life? Would you break our friendship if I don't make a career and stay poor?", Sushant looks at Ranbir expecting an answer.

"You are talking crap. Why would I break our friendship? Tell me one thing...why are you suddenly being so concerned about actors making money? Why is money on your mind?"

"Because she went away as my future didn't seem bright to her. Tell me how can career and money take precedence over love?" Sushant hits the wall behind him with his elbow.

"She may not be totally wrong", Ranbir speaks softly. "Money though not everything is definitely something. I think the girl is practical"

"Tuck off, if money is all that she wants ...I will throw it on her face, but I will never forgive her", Sushant rages.

"Calm down", Ranbir thinks it best to change the topic. "From tomorrow, I am starting my football practice would you come?"

"Not tomorrow, may be the day after tomorrow", Sushant says looking into the void.

ACTION-PACKED MORNING.

For the first time Ranbir wakes up early that day for football practice. He calls up his team and tells them to meet at Parsee Gymkhana in the neighbourhood. He reaches there a little earlier at 5.40 a.m and sits on the football, leaning against his bicycle waiting for his team, on the pavement outside the ground.

Suddenly a car screeches by. A voice, shrill and desperate, pierces the morning air, crying for help. Ranbir's eyes widen as he witnessed the scene unfold before him – a man, struggling against his captors, fighting for his freedom. In a heartbeat, Ranbir identifies the captive as scientist Mr. Kher.

Within the car, the captors have muffled Mr. Kher's cries with a cloth. Mr. Kher waves frantically trying to escape out of the car. Ranbir doesn't know how to react in such a situation He is torn between fear and action. In a second, his instincts tell him to act. He tosses the football in air and hits it hard. The velocity packed ball hits the windshield of the car. The driver panics and loses control of the car. The car dashes against the divider. By this time Ranbir's friends have arrived there.

"Help Mr. Kher, he is kidnapped" Ranbir shouts, his voice breaking through the chaos.

The team hurl their stud-shoes at the gangsters and injures them. The person holding Mr. Kher gets hit in the eye and starts bleeding. He fires a gunshot which licks Ranbir on his right leg. But Ranbir manages to punch the gangsters on his face. Soon the furious gangsters are targeted with stones.

Just as the situation seems dire, the timely arrival of a police patrolling van turns the tide. It is heartening to watch a police van arrive on the scene in time. The gangsters, now outnumbered and outmatched are forced into retreat.

Mr. Kher seizes this opportunity and break free from his captors' grasp. He sprints towards Ranbir, his relief palpable.

"Are you O.K. sir", Ranbir asks.

"I am fine son. How about you? I suppose you were shot at", Mr. Kher voices his concern.

"Ya, the bullet has liked my leg. That's it. I am fine", Ranbir remarks casually, almost shrugging off the wound.

Mr. Kher is overwhelmed by Ranbir's attitude.

"You are bleeding profusely, Beta. Let's go to the hospital", he insists, his voice laden with worry.

Meanwhile, the police chases after the fleeing car, determined to bring the culprits to justice. As the siren's wail fades into the distance, Ranbir is gently lifted from the pavement and carried to a nearby hospital.

Soon they enter the casualty ward of the R.N. Hospital. In spite of his own personal security issues the Professor carries out the admission procedure. He stays till Ranbir is laid on the bed. After that he excuses himself from the scene as he needs to go to the police station for filing F.I.R.

Sushant comes to the hospital with Ranbir's parents.

Ranbir's father is a great football enthusiast. He wants his son to be a football player but is heartbroken to see Ranbirs leg injured. He has to be assured by the doctor that the injury wasn't serious.

Sushant's stays back with Ranbir. Mr. Kher returns to Ranbir's ward surrounded with a group of commandoes. The Commandoes position themselves outside the ward, maintaining a vigilant watch. Mr. Kher enters into the room and sits near Ranbir's head.

"How is the wound?"

"It isn't a serious injury at all. I am fine", Ranbir says with all humbleness.

He introduces Sushant to him.

"This is Sushant my best friend"

Mr. Kher's warm smile extends to Sushant, and he extends his hand for a handshake. "You are really lucky to have friends like Ranbir, who are selfless"

"Yes, I know, sir", Sushant smiles at Ranbir.

Mr. Kher reaches for his coat pocket, drawing forth a gift. He hands it to Ranbir, the gleam of appreciation evident in his eyes "Here is a token of appreciation from me"

The device is a dream of any teenager. A futuristic cell phone.

The look on Ranbir's face is not to be missed. How badly he wanted a mobile. But, Ranbir hesitated.

"It looks expensive, sir, how can I take it?", Ranbir speaks without taking his gaze off the gadget.

"I am indebted to you, friend.", says Mr. Kher.

Ranbir looks at Sushant. Sushant pats his back.

Mr. Kher, a man of science and innovation, had crafted the mobile using nanotechnology. He had used nanotechnology to give the instrument a flexible body that could be re-shaped depending on the user's needs, a far cry from today's solid and chunky devices. Even the electronics inside were transparent and flexible, so the whole phone may be twisted and stretched into bracelet shapes or tablet form, and nanotech cleverness means it would even clean itself. It also functioned as a medical gadget to review the health of the user. The cell phone measured the temperature and other drastic discrepancies in the body.

The boys are awestruck. Soon Mr. Kher takes them to the Games Application and then all the other Applications take a backseat. The bed is literary transformed into a playground, and the lasers from the mobile throw 4D images on the white linen. The bed becomes a canvas for holographic displays, the room pulsating with excitement and discovery. The hospital environment momentarily fades.

Mr. Kher gives them demos. In the excitement all have forgotten that they are in hospital. The enthusiastic shouts bring in the stern Matron.

"What on earth is going on in here?", the Matron authoritative voice cut through the air, her gaze zeroing in on Sushant, "You here again, what kind of trouble are you causing now?"

Quickly, Mr. Kher intervenes, deactivating the device. "Good morning Sister, I am Mr. Kher"

"The Mr. Kher?" recognition dawns on the Matron's face. "It's an honour, sir"

"Same here"

"You here with these naughty guys? This guy in the blue shirt had created a ruckus a few days ago", the Matron said pointing to Sushant. Sushant hangs his head in shame.

"Naughty? Well, he might be naughty but he is a friend of a person who risked his life to save a stranger? Birds of feather flock together. How could he possibly be bad?"

Sushant's heart swells with gratitude as he looks at Mr. Kher. The professor's affirmation not only saves Sushant from a potentially awkward situation but also deepens his admiration for the man. He liked the man for what he did. Till now life had been a bit unfair to Sushant.

Mr. Kher narrates the kidnapping incident.

"God bless you, my children." The old matron says.

The Cloning Effect

The three bond strong and fast. The age difference doesn't seem to be a problem at all.

"Why were the gangsters after you?", curiosity burns in Ranbir's eyes..

"They wanted the formula of cloning from me. I am saying this because they have stolen my cloning machine.", Mr. Kher replies.

"Cloning, what's that?", Sushant eyes are wide with fascination. He is always intrigued by such words.

"It's a process where your duplicate is created, the duplicate is an living and breathing photocopy of you," answers Rabir.

"Wow that's interesting", Sushant's reaction is one of pure wonder.

"Hey that pretty good info. How did you come to know?", Mr. Kher is surprised to find Ranbir aware of the experiment.

"Saw your interview on 'Walk the Talk,' sir", says Ranbir.

A realization dawns on Mr. Kher as he connects the dots. "Ah, that interview might be the reason the gangsters are after me."

Sushant's curiosity is unquenchable as he leans in. "How would The Don benefit from this cloning?"

Mr. Kher explains, "The don plans to clone himself to create a double. The duplicate would then be used to confuse the police. If the authorities are convinced that they have apprehended the original Don, then his name would be struck off from the Most Wanted List thus making him a free person.

Sushant is fascinated by Mr. Kher's story. He sits on the bed with a Phew...

The gravity of the situation hung heavy in the air. Everybody realises the possibility of manipulation of technology for nefarious purposes. As the trio engages in this dialogue, the bond between them seem to deepen further.

"How do you manage to make such inventions? Sushant lets out a breath of amazement. I have issues even to by-heart basic equations.", Sushant confesses, his tone betraying a hint of vulnerability.

"Sometimes luck helps but most of the time it is the right motivation that pays", Mr. Kher says looking at the flabbergasted Sushant.

Sushant has made a statement about himself. He is grappling with a low self-esteem.

"What do you do?", Mr. Kher asks Sushant.

"Promoted to S.Y.B.Com with 3K'T"s", Sushant says as if he had by hearted it.

"So, What are your future plans?", Mr. Kher asks observing Sushant intently.

"Want to make money", is Sushant's quick response.

"Go, rob the bank then", Mr. Kher quips.

Sushant is taken aback by the answer. He looks up at Mr. Kher. He clearly hadn't expected such a response.

Looking at the frown on his face, Mr. Kher tries to clarify his perspective. "Even a prostitute earns money. Money making is not a big deal. It is important – how you make money". Mr. Kher's disposal was now serious. "Prepare yourself for hard work, don't depend on luck.

Always plan your next move". Sushant listens intently. For the first time he doesn't seem to mind being lectured by someone.

The frank words of Mr. Kher, his status, and his caring attitude impresses Sushant.

After speaking to Sushant, Mr. Kher has derived a conclusion. According to him, Sushant is depressed and grappling with his own inner battles, but who has an inherent trustworthiness and potential for growth. Moreover, he is Ranbir's friend. A person is as good as the company he keeps.

Sushant receives a call on his mobile from his mother. He has to go. He promises to come back and stay overnight in the hospital.

"Sushant seems like a nice guy". Mr. Kher opines.

"He is the heartthrob of our college. A talented dancer. Must see his fan following", saying this Ranbir shows Sushant's dance videos uploaded on YouTube.

"His moves are amazing", says Mr. Kher. "This kind of movement takes practice, dedication, hard work".

"He is super talented sir. But these days he is lost. Many reasons for it. Hope he gets back to his normal self as soon as possible". Ranbir says fingers crossed.

There's something I'd like to dicuss with you. "Mr. Kher encounters Sushant in the corridors of the hospital when he returns back. Sushant is curious.

"You know, "Mr. Kher begins, his gaze thoughtful, "I believe that every individual possesses unique qualities that can be harnessed for remarkable feats"

Sushant tilts his head, a spark of interest igniting within him. "That sounds deep. But, sir, what exactly do you mean?"

Mr. Kher leans forward, his eyes fixed on Sushant. "I've watched a few videos of you dancing, Sushant. Your performances are captivating and filled with energy and passion. It's clear that you possess an extraordinary level of discipline, focus and physical endurance."

Sushant's surprise is evident as he processes Mr. Kher's words. "Dancing is just a hobby, sir. I never really thought of it that way."

A knowing smile graced Mr. Kher's lips. "That's the beauty of potential, my young friend. Sometimes, the qualities that come naturally to us can be utilized in unexpected ways."

Sushant's curiosity deepens, his gaze fixed on Mr. Kher. "And how does this relate to me?"

Meet me on the 6th of September at this address. Sushant isn't aware of the life changing experience that is awaiting him.

The Incredible Experiment!

Sushant arrives at Mr. Kher's residence and rushes through the main gate. Suddenly, from nowhere, a commando appears, his tone firm and authoritative. He stands tall and imposing, his black attire emphasizing his trained physique.

Sushant's arm is firmly gripped by the commando, and he pulls it back with a frown. "Hey, leave my arm," he protests, not appreciating the forceful approach.

"You are trespassing. Your identity?", orders the commando.

Suddenly, Mr. Kher's voice resonates from the balcony overlooking the gate. "He is my guest," he declares, his authority carrying weight.

Giving a tough look to the commando, Sushant enters the residence, still feeling the tight grip on his arms. Mr. Kher comes in the lobby to receive him. After entering the hall, Mr. Kher shuts the door behind him. The hall is filled with antiques. Sushant is surprised that a techie like Mr. Kher could take an interest in antiques, Sushant does not like the ambience.

"So how do you like my house?", asked Mr. Kher to an unimpressed Sushant.

"Quite big but boring," says Sushant, watching a huge grandfather's clock tick loudly.

A mischievous glint dances in Mr. Kher's eyes as he seems to relish Sushant's candidness. "Then how about some excitement now," saying Mr. Kher lifts a flower pot and pressed a button at its base, the floor parts in either direction to reveal a staircase that leads underground.

Sushant's eyes widen as he watches the revelation unfold before him. "What...What is this?" he stammers, his curiosity heightened.

Mr. Kher guides him downstairs, "You are the only person to have access to this chamber."

Mr. Kher had kept that chamber a secret as he couldn't trust anyone.

Sushant starts feeling the cold due to the super cooling air conditioners. The walls are clinical and off-white giving the chamber a professional, sterile feel. The chamber are a state-of-the-art lab on nano electronics, nano chemistry, nano polymer,nano bio technology and instrumentation equipped with modern techniques like XRD, DLX, AFM, UV-VIS Spectrophotometre, and his latest invention – **The Hydro-laser machine.**

This room is a complete contrast to the drawing room which Sushant had earlier been in. Some guinea pigs could be seen squeaking in a cage. Just the ambience shouted of the experiments that had been carried out there.

The ambiance of the chamber is charged with the energy of scientific discovery. As he took it all in, Sushant felt a mixture of excitement and intrigue, a new world opening up before him.

On a raised platform some nail-sized tortoises are floating in a small circular water tank.

Mr. Kher explains their remarkable transformation, "These are actually Giant Tortoises, their original size 5 feet in length", Mr. Kher says picking one up. "Their body has been transformed to 5 centimetres."

Sushant's eyes widen in amazement as he observes the miniature creatures, Intrigued, he carefully picks up one of the miniaturized tortoises on his fingertip.

Mr. Kher playfully slaps Sushant on his back who doesn't seem to believe. And he points to a giant tortoise, a 7 feet tortoise, munching on spinach in a corner. Sushant goes near the huge tortoise.

"He is their brother", Mr. Kher proudly put his hand on the massive shell of the 350 kg. tortoise.

Sushant is not ready to believe what he is listening to. But the words are coming from Mr. Kher. Still, Sushant's mind struggles to comprehend the incredible reality unfolding before his eyes.

"This Hydro laser machine can literally transform your size and life, Yes, Literally". Says Prof. Mr. Kher smiling with confidence as he shows the huge Hydro-laser machine.

The top part of the machine replicates a mother's womb. It is a large pear-shaped tank, made of glass. Just below the transparent glass, we could see some soft white spongy stuff and also some colourless liquid. Like the fallopian tubes some pipes, releasing bubbles, could be seen immersed in the liquid. But, there is not a single skilled technician around.

"Now, here comes the deal", Mr Kher says "I have an experiment in mind, Sushant, one that requires individuals with specific attributes. The experiment involves a high level of mental and physical challenges."

Sushant's heart quickens. The idea of being part of an experiment, especially one conducted by someone of Mr. Kher's calibre, is both exhilarating and nerve-wracking.

Mr. Kher's gaze locks onto Sushant's. "I believe that your qualities as a dancer could make you an excellent candidate for this experiment. Your ability to withstand pressure, your discipline, and your mental fortitude are qualities that could contribute to its success."

"If you trust me and offer yourself for the experiment, you will be paid 1 crore just for offering your body for the experiment."

"One crore just for being a Guinea pig?" Sushant takes a moment to absorb Mr. Kher's words.

"Yes, and if anything goes wrong, resulting a harm to your body, like deformity or handicap, your family will be paid 10 crores," Mr. Kher says in a strict business tone.

Sushant does not like the word deformity but the word "1 crore" makes him think. He has faith in Mr. Kher. The offer is unbelievable. He smiles in agreement.

Mr. Kher is overjoyed because he had an opportunity to carry out an experiment on someone he could trust blindly.

"Be here on the 6th of September, at 3.00 noon. Remember to stay on liquid diet the whole day", saying this Mr. Kher hands him a list of some do's and don'ts.

Ranbir is declared fit and discharged from the hospital. He is finding it hard to kill time at home. He is glad to see Sushant coming towards him. Sushant tell him about the experiment and the offer.

The intrigue deepens as Sushant describes the Hydro-laser machine, the miniature tortoises and the astonishing offer that involves transforming one's size and life.

Ranbir listens intently, his curiosity growing with every word. The mere idea of such an experiment is mind-boggling, and the generous compensation added an irresistible element. As Sushant reveals that Mr. Kher has permitted him to discuss this only with Ranbir, a sense of privilege and trust washes over him.

"Are you thinking about it?" Ranbir finally asks, his voice tinged with anticipation.

Ranbir's question lingers in the air, the answer yet to be voiced. The duo sit there, contemplating the unknown journey that lies ahead.

THE 'U' TURN.

As the appointed day arrives, Sushant finds himself standing in front of the imposing Hydro-laser machine, its size and complexity sending shivers down his spine. The atmosphere is charged with a mix of excitement and nervous anticipation. The laboratory seems to hum with an energy of its own, the promise of a ground breaking experiment hanging in the air.

The person, in the experiment, is subjected to a combination of electrolyte solution (similar to the amniotic fluid in the uterus), and cold laser rays, which reverses the process of cell multiplication. The combination of water and laser rays reverses the effect the time may have had on cells of the body. This meant, that an aged person could get back his youth if exposed to the hydro – laser therapy. It is even possible to achieve a child or a foetus stage depending on the time of exposure of a cell to the hydro-laser rays.

The big machine is grumbling big time. The huge pear shaped glass structure towering 12 feet high is placed on a podium that resembled a rocket launcher. The machine is surrounded with laser machines suspended mid-air via cables.

As Sushant stands there, his thoughts swirl with a mixture of curiosity and anxiety. The idea of immersing himself in the electrolyte solution akin to the amniotic fluid seem both surreal and science fiction-like. Cold lasers rays, reversing cell multiplication – it is a concept that pushes the boundaries of his understanding. He couldn't help but wonder about the potential outcome of this experiment.

"Are you ready", asks Mr. Kher confidently, almost expecting a "yes" for an answer.

But something unexpected meets Mr. Kher's ears.

"No," Sushant's voice carries an undertone of doubt and apprehension. The coldness of the room seems to intensify as beads of sweat form on Sushant's forehead, despite the chill in the air. His uncertainty is palpable. "What if the experiment doesn't go as per the plan?", Sushant has his apprehensions.

"I told you that your family will be compensated with 10 Crore.", Mr. Kher replies in a cool tone.

"So there are chances that the experiment could fail, right?", Sushant tenses up.

Mr. Kher replies in a pragmatic and composed manner, "As per the laws by which we are conducting this experiment, it has a 99.99% success rate. The experiment on the tortoise was successful too. But its practicality on human being is yet to be proved. You are being paid for that 0.1% of uncertainty or risk associated with the experiment." His tone is reassuring.

The weight of the situation is evident in Sushant's expression. A mix of emotions play across his face – doubt, anxiety, and a hint of desperation. He seems torn between the promise of a significant reward and the fear of the unknown.

"If money is going to be traded for my life, and if I have an option, I would rather earn it by safe means," says Sushant almost taking a U-turn on his decision to offer himself.

Mr. Kher's voice carries a depth of emotion that was hard to miss. His words are more than just persuasive;

they resonate with genuine sentiment. "Without you I would not be able to conduct the experiment. You are the person whom I trust. As a dancer, you have more endurance capacity than an average human being; so any slight fluctuations could be endured by you. Your body composition is just perfect for the experiment. It would be hard for me to find such an athletic body, moreover, The secrecy of the experiment could also be at risk."

In that moment, it becomes clear that Mr. Kher's desire for Sushant to participate in the experiment goes beyond a mere business transaction. There is a genuine need for Sushant's involvement.

"You have an opportunity to earn and I have an opportunity to give you that opportunity. Won't you like to make the most of this. Life becomes exciting with risks, and this is a well calculated risk."

Sushant's uncertainty hung in the air, a palpable tension that reflected his internal struggle. But even as he hesitates, Mr. Kher's unwavering respect for their friendship becomes evident. " I value relations more than anything. I can't afford to lose a friend." Mr. Kher's words are laced with sincerity, "If you don't believe me, you can take your call."

Sushant could see the honesty and the earnest request in Mr. Kher's eyes. In that moment, he saw a friend who believed in him, a chance to embark on an extraordinary journey, and the scary shadow of uncertainty. The room seems to hold its breath, and time momentarily freezes.

"Yes, I will go for it", are the strong, determined words of Sushant.

Nude, unconscious body of Sushant, is immersed in a Hydro-Laser Machine. Mr. Kher's hands move with purpose, his fingers pressing buttons adjacent to the machine to initiate the experiment. The machine responds with a low hum, and cold laser lights begin to flash with intense brilliance within the water. Sushant's body could be seen disappearing in the red lights, twisting and turning in the water. The room is bathed in a surreal red glow as the process begins.

As the laser lights pulse, Sushant's body seems to twist and turn within the liquid, like a dancer lost in his rehearsal routine. The lights cast intricate patterns on his skin, and the water ripples around him in response to the machine's energy.

The hours tick by. Finally, after approximately 9 hours of intense experimentation, the machine's pulsations gradually slowed. The red glow begins to fade, and the liquid in the chamber stills. The room seems to exhale as the experiment reaches its conclusion.

Gentle mechanical arms descend into the chamber, carefully lifting Sushant's unconscious body from the liquid. He is laid on a specially designed surface. As the red glow gave way to a soft, ambient light.

"Wake up...Wake up son" Mr. Kher says. Sushant can hear these words with a soft touch on his cheeks. He opens his eyes to find an exuberant Mr. Kher trying to coax him out of sleep.

Sushant slowly wakes up to Mr. Kher's gentle words, like sunshine on a sleepy morning. His head feels foggy, like a mist in the air.

"Good morning" as he tries to speak, his voice sounds strange, like a high-pitched melody. His teenage voice is replaced by a child-like voice. He puts his hand on the throat but is further flabbergasted to find his muscular arm replaced with a baby arm.

"What the ......," he tries to get up. His legs feel like jelly, wobbling like a new born deer taking its first steps.

"Relax, relax", Mr. Kher's voice is like a soft blanket, wrapping around him to calm his racing heart.

Mr. Kher gently leads Sushant to a mirror. Sushant can't believe what he is watching. He sees a red-haired baby staring back from the mirror. He is physically transformed into a 1-year-old infant but his memory is the same as an adult!!!

Sushant's heart races like a speedy train. He touches his tiny fingers to his cheek, feeling the soft skin of a baby.

"Dear, don't make much moments as yet. Your body needs time to adjust" Mr. Kher's voice is a soothing melody, like a lullaby pacifying his worries. He tells Sushant to take things slow. Sushant nods, his baby eyes blinking with a mix of surprise and curiosity.

With time, the changes start to sink in. He is now able to smile at his own baby punk looks. But the fear hasn't subsided. "Please, change me back to my original self, sir"

"Let's call Ranbir first," suggest Mr. Kher. Mr. Kher is as excited as a child who wants to show his first painting to his friends.

Mr. Kher calls Ranbir on his cell and tells him to come at his residence.

When Ranbir arrives, he is led straight to the Chamber where Sushant is kept. But the expressions are different on Mr. Khers face this time. He is silent.

"Sir, you sounded excited when you had called me. You look worried now? Is everything okay? Ranbir's worry is palpable in his voice, his heart racing with uncertainty. Mr. Kher remains silent. He appears more grief-stricken.

"Mr. Kher, what's the matter? Please tell me.", Ranbir starts panicking.

"Everything changed in an hour", says Mr. Kher, his voice choking.

His words hang in the air like a heavy fog, and Ranbir's heart sinks. He looks in the direction Mr. Kher pointing to, and his eyes widen in shock. Underneath a white cloth lay a tiny body. Dread fills the air as Ranbir slowly lifts the cloth, revealing a small figure.

"Grrrrrrrrrrrrrrrrr....." sits up Sushant, scaring the daylights out of Ranbir.

As the cloth falls away completely, a 1-foot-tall infant sits there, laughing his heart out. Ranbir's jaw practically hits the floor. He can't believe his eyes. This little version of Sushant, laughing so innocently, is beyond anything he could have imagined.

Ranbir goes near Sushant, still not believing his eyes. He touches Sushant.

"We are successful," says Mr. Kher shaking Ranbir joyfully. Mr. Kher picks up Sushant and does a jig.

"Unbelievable!!!", exclaims Sushant, recovering from the shock..

Mr. Kher had ordered a Cheese burst pizza. He mischievously hands Sushant a bowl of Ceralac. Sushant politely puts it aside and snatches the pizza on the table.

"What, no champagne?", Sushant quips, munching on the pizza. Mr. Kher draws out the milk bottle. All the three laugh their heart out.

"To Dr. Kher," says Ranbir raising the pizza to him.

"Now I don't mind accepting this title," Mr. Kher raises his pizza too.

"How would this experiment benefit humanity?" Ranbir inquires, genuinely curious about the broader implications.

"Old people and women are going to love this," Mr. Kher says, wiping his hand on a napkin. He turns towards Ranbir. "There is a section of society who is willing to spend a fortune to get their youth back. Though people would not like to be infants, but a 60-year-old would certainly like to get back in his 30 s". This experiment has the potential to return back your youth, just like Ponds Age Miracle"

"WOW!" exclaims Ranbir, his excitement evident. As a thought crosses his mind, his face lit up even more.

"What are you thinking about?" asks Mr. Kher reading Ranbir's face.

"We would like to use your formula personally, of course, if you allow us," Ranbir says, brimming with excitement.

"Yes, tell me. How can I help you", Mr. Kher is eager to help.

Ranbir shares his heartfelt sentiments, "I fell in love with a girl. But I didn't get enough time to understand her. I ruined a possible relationship even before it started."

Mr. Kher is all ears.

"I just want to be in her company. I want to understand her, her likes, her dislikes." Ranbir says, looking at Sushant. "We would like to know what they think about us."

A warm smile spread across Mr. Kher's face, as he recognizes the depth of Ranbir's feelings.

"Something still says that we are made for each other. Life seems impossible without her.", Ranbir continues. "What better way to know her than to be in her company in the guise of a baby."

"I am game," Mr. Kher says sipping on the cola.

But Sushant, on the other hand, is frowning. Wickedly he says, "Yes, we want to be near them".

Sushant's baby face is giving out vibes of villainous intent. He is a rejected lover.

The Girls' Hostel

A knock is heard at the door. Jethi, the woman watchman, opens the door to find two adorable babies grinning up at her from a perambulator. The babies are totally drenched in rain and are draped only in napkin. The only accessories they were adorning are the lockets. Mr. Kher had installed a GPS system in it so as to keep a track of their whereabouts. Mr. Kher had a GPS screen installed in his laboratory. A green signal beep indicating the whereabouts of the babies.

Jethi calls up Miss Vaswani from her dormitory.

Miss Vaswani is Androphobic, a total male hater. And the growing number of rape cases, MMS scandles, blackmailing, molestations had asserted her belief that 'All men are dogs'. Miss Vaswani though a lovely lady, is very strict when it comes to boys. She watches the boys like a wild buffalo, ready to attack at the slightest of hint. She is strictly against her girl students, having any kind of contact with boys. Miss Vaswani is a powerful lady with a lot of administrative powers. Students are scared even to acknowledge each other in her presence. No men or even male relatives are allowed in the girls' hostel.

"Jethi, check karo baba hai ya baby hai," Miss Vasvani says, looking suspiciously at the babies.

Jethi lowers the napkins to check, "Boys."

The boys wink at Miss Vaswani. They know the effect it would likely trigger.

"My God... these boys, I tell you...take them away to orphanage immediately or .... call the police or whatever...

take them away from here now," Miss Vaswani orders sternly.

To an outsider, this reaction might have seemed extreme, but considering her androphobic tendencies, it was just another day in her world of strict regulations and firm beliefs.

Jethi is aware of Miss Vaswani's personality. She immediately dials a local police station number from her mobile as the landline in the office is out of order. But due to some connection issues, Jethi is not able to get through. The fact is Mr. Kher has set up a network jammer whereby no calls could be made out of the hostel.

"My cell is not getting the range", Jethi complains. Mrs. Vasvani tries her mobile, which fails too."

"I will keep them with me tonight," Jethi says, pulling the perambulator away from Miss Vaswani's sight towards her room on the ground floor just beside the gate.

"*Sali ne mujhe dhakka diya tha, rukh iska chashma ki tod deta hu*", mulls Sushant, looking at Jethi.

Sushant starts screaming at the top of his lungs. Jethi picks him up to calm Sushant. Sushant, without warning, catches her specks and throws it on the ground.

"You broke my spectacles," Jethi laments, "You *Badmash.*"

Sushant starts to howl.

Jethi wants to smack the boy but hold back as already he is howling in the dead of night.

The noise brings all the girls out of their room. They are in their nighties, staring from the staircases that leads to the floors above. Sushant's crying drama ends with a "WOW, What a sight!!!"

But Ranbir has his eyes fixed on Amruta, who is looking stunning in her pink gown with three white big buttons sewn on it. With other girls, she curiously watches the abandoned babies.

Two of the three buttons on her gown are left unbuttoned. In the girl's hostel, at that point in time, Amruta is half asleep and isn't even aware of the wardrobe malfunction. Genelia is standing beside her. It is two in the morning yet Genelia has her specks perched on top of her head and a book in her hand. She has tied her hair in ponytail style and has a pen going perpendicular through her hair band.

Both boys cry "Mummy!!!" in unison.

One of the hostel girls picks up Sushant. Sushant frantically tries to get off her. He lunges towards Genelia but she retracts back. Amruta who is standing next to Genelia, picks up Sushant as well.

Sushant has a nice opportunity to chide Ranbir. He catches the two buttons, one in each of his baby paw, and look at Ranbir for his reactions. Ranbir's face shows sign of uneasiness. Sushant playfully starts pulling at the buttons.

Ranbir gets down from the perambulator and crawls towards Genelia and tugs at her gown. Genelia reluctantly picks him up.

Ranbir embraces Genelia's face and kisses her on her cheeks. He turns Genelia's face and moves forward as if to kiss her on her lips. He stops and looked at Sushant for his reactions.

Sushant immediately releases the buttons. Ranbir stops his Imran Hashmi Acts.

They signal each other, "*Bhai-bhai..bhai-bhai*"

The babies stay calm in their hands. They even put the finger on their lips.

"I think you should handle the babies tonight,' Miss Vaswani says , "They seem to keep quite in your company, take them in your rooms"

The babies are brought into the room and kept on the sofa.

"*Chalo inko doodh pilate hai*", says Genelia. This sentence freezes them for a second. Heaven knows what came to their mind.

"Par dood to khatam ho gaya hai," Amruta checks the milk bottle in the fridge.

"Their mom must have fed them well before leaving," saying this, Genelia starts reading the book.

Amruta makes a vegetable soup and feeds them, and then goes into the kitchen to finish cleaning. Genelia continues to immerse herself in reading. Finding the girls busy, Sushant quietly opens his heart shaped locket and speaks in it. "Sir, can you hear me?"

"Yes Sushant, Is everything fine?" Mr. Kher asks.

"Yes Sir, we are with them, in the room", Sushant speaks tongue in cheek.

"Don't misbehave, kids," Mr. Kher laughingly warns them.

'Ha ha ha ....ok bye sir, we will keep on reporting," saying this, Sushant hangs up.

Amruta sings a beautiful lullaby to the babies, "*Aao Tumhe Chand Pe Le Jaye*"

Is the lullaby soothing or is it the strain of the day? Before they know it, both of them fall asleep.

LOVE BLOOMS!

Bright sunshine lights the room. Ranbir is up, and the first thing he wants to do was to use washroom.

He searches for the washroom. He yanks at a door but the door opens to the kitchen. He opens another door, which opens to the hall. It almost looks as if Ranbir would not be able to control, when at last he finds the toilet. He removes his napkin and climbs up the commode.

"What a bliss", thought Ranbir, relieving himself.

"Bang!!! The bathroom door opens, and in come Genelia. She is shocked to find Ranbir on the commode.

"Commode mei gir jate to??? She screams and picks up Ranbir.

Ranbir is embarrassed to the hilt. He covers his face.

Sushant, who is sitting awake on the bed, falls rolling on the floor laughing.

A fellow student from the neighbour, who has taken up stitching classes as a hobby, comes and hands over two baby dresses that she has woven. Soon, Ranbir is dressed in light blue tunic and looks the most adorable baby. Sushant is dressed up in red tunic matching his head colour. He literally looks on fire.

After instructing the girls to hand over the children to police station, Miss Vaswani leaves the hostel for some meeting. She is to return only by evening. Jethi is also accompanying her.

The news spread like wildfire. It means it is time to for the girls to let their hair down. Suddenly the neighbouring room of

Genelia starts emitting sound level well beyond the permissible levels. All the girls gathered in the room to shake a leg.

The room of Genelia and Amruta, has a different atmosphere. Both the girls are preparing to hand over the babies to the police station.

After dressing up the babies, Amruta decide to change her clothes. Amruta pulls up her gown.

"Hey, not in front of the babies, go in the bed room", Genelia almost shouts.

"Why? They are just kids", Amruta replies.

"Don't know why, but these kids suddenly go hungry when we change", Genelia answers quite perplexed.

"How do you know?", Amruta asks, surprised.

"They shout '*Du Du..... Du Du*', Genelia answers.

So leaving the kids in the hall, both of them go into the bedroom to change.

The volume pumps up in the adjacent room. Sushant's feet involuntarily start thumping to the music. He runs out of the room and enters the neighbour's room. The girls are dancing on the floor adjacent to the bed in the hall. Sushant, in his baby avatar, climbs up on the bed. Sushant walks briskly at the centre of the bed and suddenly enters into a slow-motion mode.

"Whoa!!! Did you see that?" a girl shouts, her eyes as wide as saucers.

"Oh my god!!!" say others in disbelief.

The track plays on. The dance continues, Soon Genelia and Amruta come looking for Sushant, to find Sushant doing slow motion on the bed. All the girls are spell bound.

But the scene is different with Genelia. Tears started flowing from Genelia's eyes. She runs back to her room and shuts herself in the bedroom. Amruta picks up Sushant and returns into the room to find the bedroom locked.

"Open the door Gen, what's the matter? Why are you crying?" Amruta asks puzzled.

Wiping her tears off, Genelia let Amruta in.

"Is everything ok?", Amruta asks concerned.

"You have always seen me as a tough person. But the fact is my heart cries in pain for someone," Genelia confesses.

Confused and concerned, Amruta sits down beside her "Who is he?"

Genelia takes a deep breath, her voice soft but laden with emotion. "Do you remember I had told you about a boy who had lied to me, to be friends with me".

"Ya, and you had warned him, right?"

"Yes, I did rebuke him, but the fact of the matter is I can't take my mind off him. I really like him. I want to forget him but somehow I am reminded of him. Even this baby reminds me of him," Genelia confesses, with a tear in her eyes.

Amruta listens attentively, realising the depth of Genelia's feelings, and then says "You mean....you actually like him? But if you think that you can't take him out of your mind and if he is a nice person, why don't you continue with the friendship. Staying away will disturb you both".

"No, it is important to be away because proximity breeds affection. Sushant is careless about his life. He doesn't have clear career goals. And this will create problems in our future life. I am ambitious but Sushant is like a ship without a sail. Soon, the status difference would start surfacing, and I fear that our relationship would end just like it did in my parent's case."

"What happened to your parents?"

"My parents are divorced. They had a love marriage. My mother is a doctor and my father earns by doing odd jobs every day. The difference in status made my father an alcoholic. Not a single day passed without heated arguments and physical abuse."

"According to psychology, this kind of conflict can often arise when there are significant status differences in a relationship", Amruta adds.

"Exactly, I'm worried that history might repeat itself if I get too close to Sushant. I can't let my heart rule over my head when I know that our differences might eventually drive us apart. But the fact is I really love him from the bottom of my heart. Somehow he thinks I tried to harm him and he is away from me. Good for him to hate me, but the fact is my heart aches for him."

"OHHHH GOD !!! ...', Sushant exclaims from behind the door, unable to hold back his emotions. Both the boys had been eavesdropping on their conversation. Tears well up Sushants eyes. He run into the kitchen. Ranbir follows him and hugs him in a tight embarace. Sushant could not control his tears.

"She loves you so much!", Ranbir whispers reassuringly. "And you had wrong impression about her."

"True, I literally had a wrong impression about her." Sushant nods, wiping his tears, feeling euphoric.

The two girls come out of their room still unaware that he babies are eavesdropping.

"Amruta, have you ever experienced something where someone seems so amazing that it takes over your heart and mind?" Genelia asks curiously.

"There was this cute guy once, he helped me on the bus. He actually proposed to me. But, c'mon, love doesn't happen like this. I mean... you meet someone in the morning and get proposed in the evening. This cannot be love......right? Though I must admit he had something in him that really drew me in." Amruta says.

Sushant glances at Ranbir. Ranbir is speechless. Sushant's analysis was correct – rushing into things had ruined a potential relationship.

What a day in the lives of the two, to find that the one they loved, loved them too!!!

One Night Adoption

Genelia receives a call on her cell, “Hello Mamaji” she says cheerfully.

“Hello beta!!!,” greets Dr. Johnny. “I was passing this way, thought of meeting you. Can you come out of your hostel gate?”

“*Mamaji*, actually I am on my way out. We’re going to the police station,” Genelia replies.

“Is everything all right?” Johnny panics.

“No need to worry *Mama*, it is just that we are handing our babies to the police,” Genelia winks at Amruta. Amruta pushes Genelia playfully. Genelia always played pranks on her uncle.

“*Tumhare bacche*, what do you mean?” enquires Johnny confused.

“Hold on mama I will come down and explain,” saying this Genelia hangs up the phone.

“What does your mama do?”, Amruta asks, climbing down the staircase.

“My Mama is a child specialist, but he doesn’t have any children himself”

The car is parked few metres away from the hostel. The two babies are trolleyed near the car.

“What beautiful babies!!!” Johnny says pulling their cheeks. His tanned sunburnt skin is a contrast against the soft pink skin of the babies.

Ranbir is seized by a series of sneezes.

"Hey this cute gentleman seems to have caught a cold. Let's take him to my clinic first.", Johnny suggests.

"Yeah, once they are handed over to police, we wouldn't know how they would be treated", Amruta is as caring as ever.

Soon they arrive at their house-cum-clinic. The door is opened by Johnny's wife, Mohini, who is a little overzealous South Indian lady.

"*Aiyooooooo........kitna pyara baccha ji.... Tumhara hai kya????*", Mohini almost screams lifting Ranbir from Amruta's arm.

She screams so loudly that normal babies would have gone deaf. Thank god these babies could stick their fingers in their ears and save their eardrums.

"No chachi, somebody left them in the hostel, we are taking them to police station" Genelia makes things clear.

"Come on in," said Mohini in her usual hyper mode and locks the door behind them. "I'll get water for you."

She hurriedly goes into the kitchen with Ranbir and calls her husband inside. "Aiyoo... kitne pyare gore gore bacche hai. I want them. We will adopt them," says Mohini in her funny South Indian accent.

"WTF", Ranbir babbles.

"How can we keep them?" Johnny explains" They are to be taken to the police station."

"Mataji came in my dreams yesterday and offered me two '*laddus,*' these are those two laddus," says Mohini trying hard to convince Johnny.

"This is a police case. Somebody had left the kids outside the girl's hostel. We may get into trouble", Johnny says.

"*Aiyoo*...After all these years, we never had a child. Now that one has come, you're taking him away. Please, let's keep these children for today at least", Mohini pleads with a pout.

"O.k. I will see what I can do', saying this Johnny carries Ranbir and goes into the in-house clinic. He places Ranbir on the bed.

Ranbir communicates with Sushant in a sign language. Sushant is horrified.

"The child has to be kept under observation. He is having severe cough. The cough could be problematic if not treated now," Johnny lies, removing the statoscope around his neck.

"But is it serious, Uncle?" asks Amruta.

"Even small thing could be serious if not taken seriously", Johnny says.

"But what shall we say to the Dean?", Genelia asks.

"Tell her that they were hospitalised for some medical reason. Nobody can object to that," Johnny provides solution.

"Please start the medication. We don't want any complications due to delay," Amruta says, who is as gullible as ever.

"Let the other baby stay here too. One will panic not seeing the other," Johnny suggests.

"O.K. we will inform our dean about this. We will come back tomorrow," says Genelia as they kiss the babies goodbye. The boys, for once, didn't like their goodbye kisses.

Mohini is on cloud nine as she gets to keep the babies with her. Her hyper acts catch momentum.

"I wish one was a girl," she says looking at the two baby boys.

"This one is so cute, almost like a girl," says Johnny, pulling Ranbir's cheeks. How Ranbir hated that.

"Let's dress him up like one," is Mohini's idea. Ranbir's wants to use the 'F' word.

She opens the cupboard and pulls out at least a dozen frocks. She spreads them on bed, and the couple initiate the process of transforming Ranbir into a lovely baby doll.

"What's happening here. Enough of this transformation business. I don't want to be turned into a girl now.", Ranbir panics.

"Don't mind, yaar. You would look ravishing", Sushant laughs.

"Get lost,.... find a way out of here", Ranbir starts searching for a way out of the room.

"Don't panic, we will speak to Mr. Kher on microphone". Sushant calms Ranbir showing his locket around his neck.

"Do you think the babies look a little tired", Mohini asks. The stress was obvious on the babies' faces.

"Let's give them a nice steam shower," Johnny suggests.

"Shall I remove this locket?" says Mohini, tugging at the heart shaped locket dangling around Sushant's neck.

"O.k. remove it. I will keep them in the safe," Johnny agrees.

Both the babies look at each other in bewilderment. Johnny takes the two lockets and puts them in a safe. The babies are put in the tub. They aren't able to laugh on their naked bodies anymore.

After the steam and bath session, they are placed on the bed. Sushant is made to wear the boy's clothes, but for Ranbir, the couple goes ahead with their plan.

After 30 minutes of make-up, Ranbir is a sight to be seen. His hair is carefully plaited. His entire forehead is covered with a big south Indian bindi. Kajal flows out of his eyes. Extra talcum powder makes his body shine like a tube light.

"How beautiful our children look!!!" admires Mohini. Johnny smiles, taking her into his arms, "Happy dear?" Mohini nods.

Sushant pulls up Ranbir's skirt, "You look sexy." Ranbir pulls it down.

Here on the GPS screen, Dr. Kher notices the flashing lights flashing but stationary at a point. Mr. Kher is worried as the lights are not blinking over the girl's hostel.

Mr. kher picks up his mobile to communicate with the babies via microphone in their lockets, but the babies don't respond. This situation heightens Mr. Kher's anxiety.

He calls up again to find no response. Now Mr. Kher has no option but to meet Genelia or Amruta. As it is night Mr. Kher decides to go the next day, as meeting the girls at an unearthly hour could have created suspicion and unwanted attention.

The babies try to search for the locker so they can access the microphone but in vain. Mohini doesn't let them out of sight even once. They couldn't even access her mobile.

Here, the couple are enjoying their newly acquired parenthood. Johnny empties his shopping bag filled with Ceralac, gripe water, Johnson and Johnson soap etc.

It is dinner time. Mohini has prepared some mouth-watering dishes for celebration. Jalebis, Rasam, Steaming Rice, Basundi, mango pickle, Dal tadka adorned the dish. The good food aura spread in the air. At once the babies found their stomach growling for food.

She takes the babies and sits beside Johnny. She serves Johnny, gets up and goes inside the kitchen. The babies expect some clean shiny dish where they could be served the appetising dinner. But Mohini returns with two bowls of Ceralac.

"Hey, are we going to eat this?", Ranbir's sign language expresses his pathetic looks.

Sushant just slaps his own forehead in disappointment.

Soon the spoon enters the greasy Ceralac and heads towards Sushant first. Sushant retreats backwards.

"*Mera accha baccha, chalo khana kha lo,*" Mohini force-feeds Sushant.

"Yuck", out comes the cerelac.

"*Chi ganda bacha,*" saying this, Mohini collects all the Cerelac around his mouth and feed again.

" AAAAhhh", comes out the Cerelac again.

Watching Sushant's plight, Ranbir starts running around the house.

"Aiyooo ....catch them", screams Mohini.

Adjusting his lungi, Johnny get up and runs behind the babies.

Ranbir creeps below the bed. Sushant keeps running around the house in circles. Mohini runs behind Ranbir, Cerelac bowl in one hand.

"Aiyoo, rat will eat you," says Mohini and pulls out Ranbir from below the bed.

Sushant decides to hide in the fridge. He has opened it but Johnny just manages to take a hold of him before he enters into it. Panting, they both bring them back to eat the food. Johnny places them on his lap and handcuffs their hand with his grip. "Now feed them."

The guys have no option but to complete their share of Cerelac, while the sumptuous meal lay in front of them.

Soon the couple too have their food. Johnny removes a book of alphabets for children. Soon Johnny starts showing the animal pictures. "A for Apple, B for ball."

Before he could complete C for Cat, both the babies start crying.

"I will act like a cat", says Mohini. So Mohini starts mimicking like a cat to make it more fun for the babies. She goes on her forehands and starts mewing.

"Come my cat," Johnny says.

"Mewww mew", Mohini caresses Johnny like a cat.

"D for dog', says Johnny with a mischievous smile, "Bowww bow". Soon the couple mimics a cat-dog fight. The babies are so bored of their acting that they themselves climb into the palanquin. The babies lay there motionless, their eyes closed.

"The babies are asleep, good", smiles Johnny "Baby sitting is quite a task ..uff... now for some romantic private moments to ourselves!".

Johnny croons a romantic song for his wife. Like a heroine from an old film, Mohini starts dodging Johnny who comes near her. The couple started running around the palanquin, smiling and laughing.

"*Aiyooo*...babies will see," Mohini blushes and run towards the bed. Johnny follows, picking up his lungi.

Soon the love birds are in an embrace. And yes, they have an audience too, as the two babies have put their head up from the palanquin and are watching the couple, their eyes wide; mouth open.

"*Aiyoo ... ye baccho ko bhi abhi jagna tha*", saying this Johnny quickly gets up and tries to coax them into sleeping again. The babies act asleep. Johnny goes back to his wife. No sooner is he comfortable with his wife, then the babies start staring at them once again.

Irritated, Johnny pulls the cart out into the hall and tries to sweet-talk them into sleeping again. The cupid has stuck. He just wants to get back to his wife. The babies fall asleep. Wasting no time, Johnny runs to his bed. He is desperate. Taking a blanket, he goes back into action, but lo.............. the two babies are standing at the end of the bed, watching them from a real close-up.

"Thank god we don't have children", are the words of Johnny before gulping down some sleeping pills.

THE KIDNAP

Mr. Kher drives to the girl's hostel. The tension and a feeling of guilt are obvious on his face. He enters the gate of the girl's hostel, where he is stopped by the Jethi.

"Sorry Sahebji, girls' hostel....please give your message to me," Jethi speaks politely looking at Mr. Kher's disposition.

"Please inform Amruta Sahastrabudhhe that her uncle has come to meet her," Mr. Kher requests.

Jethi checks a register and dialled Amruta on intercom "Your uncle wants to speak to you."

"Hello", Amruta picks up the call.

"Is this Amruta?", Mr. Kher's voice chokes.

"Speaking"

"Want to speak to you about the babies", Mr. Kher whispers, as Jethi is busy stopping other visitors.

Amruta panics as she thinks that Mr. Kher is a government official, "Are you from police?"

"No, Pease meet me at the bus stop right now, I would explain everything", Mr. Kher implores. Genelia accompanies Amruta and arrive at the bus stop.

Mr. Kher drives to the girl's hostel. The tension and a feeling of guilt is obvious on his face. He enters the gate of girl's hostel; where he is stopped by the Jethi.

"Sorry saab, girls hostel....give your message to me", the Jethi speaks politely looking at Mr. Kher's disposition.

"Please inform Amruta Sahastrabudhhe that her uncle has come to meet her", Mr. Kher requests.

Jethi checks a register and dials Amruta on intercom "Your uncle wants to speak to you"

"Hello", Amruta picks up the call.

"Is this Amruta?", Mr. Kher's voice chokes.

"Speaking"

"Want to speak to you about babies", Mr. Kher whispers restlessly, as Jethi is busy stopping other visitors.

Amruta panics as she thinks that Mr. Kher is a government official, "Are you from police"

"No, Please meet me at the bus stop right now, I would explain everything", Mr. Kher says.

Amruta accompanies Genelia to the bus stop.

Meanwhile, Johnny drives down to the girls' hostel with the babies in the back seat. He has tied cello tapes on their mouth. From a distance, Johnny watches the girls talking to some stranger. He goes to them.

"Hey, hey, hold on a minute! Take these troublemakers back, please! ...I have never come across such babies in my life.", Johnny interrupts, a mixture of bewilderment and appeal in his voice.

"What happened Mama?", Genelia inquires.

"These chaps have learnt to give bad words even before they have learnt to talk.", Johnny sounds hyper, just like his wife. "They have been using foul language from the time they have woken up this morning. I can totally understand why their parents must have decided to go on an extended vacation"

"These are no ordinary babies", Genelia exclaims with a hint of annoyance, glaring at the babies.

"What do you mean?", Johnny asks puzzled.

In the meantime, Mr. Kher opens the door of the car and picks up the palanquin. He removes the cello tapes from their mouth and unties their hands. The babies look like twins. Both are wearing long-white T-shirts-red stripe and a white monkey cap. The lady seems to have given up on the idea of dressing Ranbir like a baby girl.

Mr. Kher finds Ranbir's body a little warm. "This guy has a temperature; I have to give him septromicin immediately," says Mr. Kher.

Amruta immediately touches his forehead but after watching Genelia's tough glance retreats back.

"Just watch the other guy while I buy this one the tablet," saying this Mr. Kher carries Ranbir and goes in search of pharmacy nearby. The pharmacy store is a few yards away in the by-lane unseen from place where Sushant faces tough looks from Genelia.

"I am sorry, as always," says Sushant to Genelia, his eyes down cast.

"Holy smoke!", Johnny is dumbfounded.

"There you are again. You guys will never change, how right I was...", Sushant faces the music.

A SUV stops in front of the pharmacy. Seven people dressed in black storm in. Brandishing their AK-47 rifles, they threaten people around. Before Mr. Kher can react, he is blindfolded. He embraces Ranbir in a tight grip. Both of them are kidnapped.

Here, the rebuking continues for a full 5 minutes.

"Stop it Genelia. He seems to have realised his mistake.", Amruta interrupts.

"Why are they taking so long to return? It is almost 20 minutes," says Johnny.

"Call Mr. Kher on 9653486478," says Sushant, glad to have a diversion of topic.

Johnny dials the number."Mobile is switched off," he says, worried.

❤❤❤

The Secret Farmhouse

After two hours, the SUV enters a village-like place. The kaccha road has many farmhouses along it. The SUV enters a farmhouse with compound walls of at least 18 feet, having barbed wires at the top. The farmhouse is seven times bigger than any house in the neighbourhood. It is a three-storey structure, with only the upper storey visible from outside the compound walls. And if two main gates are not enough to discourage visitors, opaque windows shield the inside. All the security personnel have accommodation on the first floor, while the don occupies the top floor. The farmhouse is too humble to be recognised as an international don's hideout.

The two are brought inside an experimentation room situated on the ground floor. The interior of the room is a stark contrast to the exterior of the farmhouse. It is a sophisticated Hi-tec laboratory. Fully furnished with the state of the art instruments. There at the centre of various instruments lay the metallic cloning machine, confiscated from Mr. Kher's laboratory during his earlier kidnapping.

The cloning machine is encased in a polished metallic shell, reflecting the surrounding lights like a futuristic masterpiece. The surface is adorned with buttons, screens, and panels, each serving a specific purpose in the complex process of replication.

Clusters of cables and wires connect the machine to various instruments and devices, creating a web of connections that resemble the veins of life itself.

The heart of the cloning machine lies in its inner chamber, a place where the magic of replication takes place. This chamber is carefully designed to provide an environment that nurtures the growth of cells and genetic material. It's a controlled space where temperature, humidity, and other variables are meticulously adjusted to create the optimal conditions for the cloning process.

Monitoring systems keep a watchful eye on every step, ensuring that the process unfolds flawlessly.

Mr. Kher is made to sit on a chair. The baby is placed on a table before him.

"Welcome Mr. Kher, finally, time has brought us face to face," Mr. Denzongpa's voice echoes in the room, reminiscing the grudges they had in their college days.

Dr. Denzongpa had been an exceptional student, always striving to compete with Mr. Kher. But Mr. Kher was naturally more gifted. Due to this Dr. Denzongpa was jealous of him. Dr. Denzongpa was poor and had badly vied for the scholarship that was to be declared that day.

(Thirty Years Ago)

"God, please get me this scholarship," Denzongpa prayed in a dark corner of the college that he considered lucky for him.

"Hey, what are you doing here?", chuckled Aarif, their mutual friend. "Chanting?"

"I have to get this scholarship and I will get it", Denzongpa said, pushing Aarif as he moved from there.

"It's going to be Mr. Kher again. You don't stand a chance," chided Aarif.

"Only time will tell", Denzongpa gave a scornful look.

"Yes, just one hour".

The results were posted on the board. Majority of the crowd celebrated their passing grades, but Denzongpa had his eyes on the scholarship list and the list displayed the name of Anil Kher.

"This is unfair. I had put in my best effort. How can I not get the scholarship?" vented Denzongpa to his close friend.

"It's not you who has lost. It is Mr. Kher who has won. That chap is genius," said Denzongpa's close friend.

"Cut it out , don't praise him", Denzongpa warned him.

"OK. Fine, but the fact remains," said his friend, which angered Denzongpa further.

Denzongpa approached the professors with desperation evident in his eyes. "Sir, just lost the scholarship by a few marks, could you help me, I beg of you"

"Sorry, but nothing could be done now. The results are out", said the professor.

"I am too poor, can't afford the fees," Denzongpa pleaded again.

"What can I do? You should have brought the required grade, sorry can't help"

"Sir, I will have to leave college."

"It's your lookout," was a cold reply from the professor.

Heartbroken, Denzongpa ran to the corner spot and was inconsolable. After staying there for a while, he moved towards canteen to have a sip of water. His eyes were red, and throat parched with thirst. Denzongpa enters the canteen to find Mr. Kher already seated with his friends on chair surrounding a huge round table. Ashamed, Denzongpa pretended ignorance and started drinking the tap water.

"So Denzongpa, have your prayers been answered?", chided Aarif again.

"You never participated in sports just to get academic grade but see what you got. And here is Mr. Kher, a natural talent, an all-rounder," said another friend raising Mr. Kher's hand.

"Stop it guys, you are being rude", Mr. Kher interrupted them. Just then, a cauldron full of oily noodles spilled on the table before him. It was followed by a burning stove. Before anybody could realize what was happening, Aarif could be heard shouting of help. He was engulfed in flames.

There was one pandemonium in the canteen. An ambulance was called for. But it was too late. Aarif succumbed to his injuries. Denzongpa was not traceable from that day.

(Back to the present)

"*Safar mei koi taklif to nahi hui*", grins Dr. Denzongpa.

"*Nahi taklif to ab ho rahi hai, tumhe aazad dekhke.* It doesn't surprise me that you are working for a person with an anti-national interest.", says Mr. Kher as he recollects the horrendous incident in which he had lost his dear friend.

"Don't call me anti-national, call me power hungry. I do everything for money. Remember the way I was treated for being poor.", Dr Denzongpa says fuming with anger.

"Don't let the poverty blanket hide the culprit in you," says Mr. Kher raising his voice. "Your short-temperedness has caused losses to you and everybody; you are one talent wasted.

"Yes, I am a great talent but surely not wasted. This talent is going to make me a billionaire", said Dr. Denzongpa in a gruff tone. "Mr. Kher, share your secret of cloning. It would make me rich and even save your life"

"Do you think I would help you in your anti-national activity? I am ready to suffer any consequences, but I shall not part with the cloning secret." Mr. Kher asserts forcefully.

"If by sunset you don't cooperate with us, you are going to be one talent wasted, and this child that you are carrying, whoever he is, would never witness the pleasures of youth". Saying this, Dr. Denzongpa leaves the chamber.

Now, only one security personnel is in the experimentation room. He handcuffs Mr. Kher, leaving the child on the table as nobody knows of the child's reality.

"Wish I could talk to Sushant,", Ranbir laments.

As luck would have it, the guard receives a call on his mobile. After speaking on it, he keeps it on the table in front of Mr. Kher's chair. He removes his Ak 47 and starts wiping it with a cloth. Ranbir's eyes sparkle with a glimmer of opportunity.

Silently, he crawls towards it, and picks it up in his baby hands.

The guard keeps his rifle aside and pulls the mobile out of Ranbir's hands. Ranbir starts crying. The guard thinks for a moment and hands back the mobile. He does not consider a two-year child to be a threat. Over and above, he wants peace. The guard hands him back the mobile.

When the guard gets back to his rifle cleaning, Ranbir skillfully texts a message on Amruta's cell which says 'Dis iz Ranbir. Kidnapped. Don't rply on diz no. ; Location unknown'.

Amruta reads out the message in shock. Everybody is a worried lot.

"Let's inform the police," Johnny suggests.

"No, it would spell more trouble for all of us," says Sushant.

"But we need to take some action," Genelia says.

Sushant takes a moment to think. "Right now, I could only think of Mr. Kher's faithful Commandoes. They are trained for rescue operations. We can coordinate with them to track Mr. Kher's location using GPS system installed in his experimentation room. If the Don's team isn't aware of Ranbir's true identity, they wouldn't remove his locket which has the GPS installed in it"

The group exchange glances, realizing that this might be their best shot at rescuing Mr. Kher and Ranbir from the clutches of danger.

Johnny drives all of them to Mr. Kher's house. The car is stopped at the gate by a group of Commandoes. The Commando chief asks for identity.

"Sir, I am Sushant, remember I had an argument with you four days ago", Sushant is breathing heavily." Remember you had stopped me at the entrance." The words straight form the baby's mouth, flummoxed the commando.

"His physical appearance is the result of an experiment carried out by Mr. Kher," Genelia jumps in to explain looking at the perplexed commando.

"Yeah...yeah but how do I believe it's that same boy," the commando asks, still not coming to terms with reality.

"Sir, you saw me enter the bungalow on 6th of September, but did you see me leave?",

"No"

"That's because I was transformed into a baby and discreetly taken out by Mr. Kher from a secret exit that even you are not aware of." Sushant reveals.

"Hmmm," the Commando chief tries recollecting if he had seen the boy leaving.

"Mr. Kher is kidnapped, his life is in danger. If you allow me, I can show you the secret chamber and the G.P.S machine installed. It will help us locate Mr. Kher and the other baby," Sushant urgently explains.

"Mr. Kher, I tell you", mumbles the upset vice Commando, shaking his head partly in astonishment and partly in anger.

"Let them in, let us see if what they say holds water," orders the Commando chief to his staff. Johnny carries Sushant in his arms. All of them enter the house. After passing through the hall, they reach a flower pot. Sushant instructs the commando chief to lift it and press the button at its base. The floor split open, revealing a staircase leading underground. All climb down the staircase.

"There's the G.P.S. machine!" Sushant says, pointing with his baby fingers. Surely, a bright green cursor blinks at a location not far away from the outskirts of Mumbai.

"The Don is an international terrorist who has been in hiding for the last ten years. His desperation to be a free man would now lead to his arrest!" says the Chief Commando. "Now that we know his location, we have to devise a foolproof plan and capture him dead or alive."

"Mr. Kher is an asset to our country. We will put in our best efforts to ensure his safe return", asserts the vice Commando.

"The planning has to be made with the utmost caution, as any wrong move could endanger the life of Mr. Kher and the baby. It is very important to understand the interior of the farmhouse so as to device a foolproof strategy of attack," the Chief Commando chief says.

"But how would we know about the internal structure of the farmhouse?", questions the Vice commando.

"Sir, I can use my physical appearance to our benefit. I will try to enter the bungalow and video shoot the interiors. I will send the video on your mobile," suggests an excited Sushant.

"Great idea, provided you don't get caught", The Commando chief says.

"But how will he enter without being seen?", Johnny has his apprehensions.

"Hmmm...let's work out a plan," the Chief commandoes suggests. The Commando team starts working on a plan. They name the operation 'Strike'.

Operation Begins

In the guise of a milk supplier, Johnny carries a 10-litre steel milk container and knocks at the gates of the farmhouse. Two security personnel are standing guard on the gate, and one of them stops Johnny"

"What do you have there, buddy?" the first guard inquires, eyeing the steel milk container, his stance rigid at the gate.

"I got a call from here, someone ordered milk," Johnny lies confidently.

"Check it," the first guard instructs his colleague at the entrance.

"No need to verify, the extra milk is likely for the baby," the other guard deduces.

Johnny hands over the milk container and leaves, successfully gaining initial access to the premises as part of their plan.

The first guard peeps into the container, confirming that it is indeed filled with milk. Satisfied, they carry the container inside the store room situated on the top floor of the three-story farmhouse. This room is conveniently located next to the Don's resting area.

Inside the store room, there is a door, but it remains unlocked for easy access. After the guard leaves; the lid of the container appears to slowly levitate itself. Sushant cautiously peeps out from the container with an oxygen mask around his face. Removing his mask, he climbs down the milk container and peeps out of the store room. He walks down the corridor of the third floor, milk draping down his baby body. He walks towards the adjacent room to find The Don talking to Denzongpa, completely unaware of his presence.

Suddenly, some foot steps are heard. These are the guards on patrol for the terrace area. They are coming up. Sushant spots a blue bucket placed in the corridor and quickly pulls it over him.

One of the guards pauses on his way to terrace. He approaches the bucket. He removes his walkie-talkie and orders. "Clean up this sticky liquid in front of the store room, now." The guard then moves up on the terrace. Sushant raises the bucket just enough to peep out and assess the situation.

"Request him for the last time to cooperate, if still he doesn't buck, shoot the baby in front of him," the Don is heard giving orders to Dr. Denzongpa

"As you say, sir", saying this Dr. Denzongpa leaves the room and climbs down the stairs. Quickly Sushant comes out of the bucket and follows Dr. Denzongpa. He removes the mobile, hidden in his nappy, and starts shooting the area as he toddles behind Dr. Denzongpa.

Just like the top floor, the second floor has three rooms on one side with a long passageway in front of them. Sushant peeps into one of the rooms and finds six guards resting there. These are the guards who would soon relieve the guards on duty. He films that. A guard on duty climbs on the second floor and notices the baby peeping into the room and runs towards him. Sushant tactfully hides his cell in his nappy again.

"You lil chap, how did you come up?" saying this he carries Sushant in the laboratory on the ground floor. Sushant's pulse has exceeded the normal limit. Thankfully, the guard has mistaken him for the baby on the ground floor.

"Were you asleep? This guy had been roaming on the upper floor," admonishes the second-floor guard to the guard inside the laboratory.

"What nonsense. The chap is sitting there," saying this the guard inside the laboratory turns back to check Ranbir, but Ranbir, in time, has jumped from the table to hide beneath it just in time. Confusion clouds the laboratory guard's face as he scans the room around. Confused, the guard from the laboratory apologizes to the guard from the second floor and puts Sushant on the table in front of Mr. Kher.

As Sushant is placed on the table, he glances at Mr. Kher with a mix of urgency and determination, knowing that every second counts in their high-stakes mission.

Dr. Denzongpa is seen coming out of a toilet built inside the laboratory. He approaches Mr. Kher.

"The Don has given me the order to kill this baby if you don't cooperate now. Make your decision right now, or I will shoot this baby" with a final glance at Mr. Kher, he calls over the guard, ready to carry out the ominous command.

Sushant, the baby, locks eyes with Mr. Kher, a silent message passing between them. Sushant nods.

"Don't harm the baby, I will do as you say," Mr. Kher replies reading Sushant's facial expression.

Dr. Denzongpa's lips curls into a triumphant smile, his satisfaction evident. "Wow, that's a good decision. At last, knowledge yields to power."

"Let me take a good nap before starting on the project to be mentally alert." requests Mr. Kher.

"Very well," Dr. Denzongpa agrees, his tone is filled with anticipation. I'll be back in two hours. This is going to be a big day for all of us!"

After Dr .Denzongpa leaves, Mr. Kher picks up Sushant in his arms and pretends to fall asleep. Sushant cuddles up to Mr. Kher. The guard too has loosened the vigil after listening to the positive affirmations of Mr. Kher.

Their feigned sleep gives them an opportunity to converse without arousing suspicion. Sushant whispers in Mr. Kher's ears. "Our Commandoes are waiting, want instruction from us. They would launch an attack once they have an idea the idea of the interior of this place and our location. I have recorded some footage".

Mr. Kher's eyes light up with anticipation. "You did?"

"Yes, Only of the top floor and the second floor. Unfortunately, I was picked up in the middle of the shooting"

Sushant shows him the recorded video clips.

"We are now on the ground floor. I need to video shoot this room and the area outside it." Saying this, Sushant hits the send button to send the earlier recorded footage.

"Good", Mr. kher says.

"Oh Shit!!! Battery is low", panics Sushant. But thankfully the video clip is sent in time along with a message attached to the video that says 'These are the interiors of the top and the second floor. Please await footage of the ground floor where we are held captive.'

The guard is obsessed with his rifle; he picks it up for cleaning once more. Sushant watches the guard busy with cleaning and slides down under the table where Ranbir is hiding, they embrace each other. "*Bhai Bhai ...bhai bhai.*"

With a sense of urgency, Sushant continues, "It's action time. Commandoes are waiting to launch attack, but first they need to familiarize themselves with this place so as to devise an attack plan. I have managed to capture a good footage of top floor, where Don's resting room is, and the second floor, where security guards rest. Now, we need to provide them with the footage of ground floor."

"You stay here, I will manage that", Ranbir says. "The battery of your cell seems to be almost down but I still have the guard's mobile", saying this he quietly climbs upon the table.

Just then, the guard in the laboratory approaches Mr. Kher, "Any special order for dinner?"

"Nothing," says Mr. Kher instantly, but on second thought, he orders a Pizza, "I am quite hungry get more of everything."

As the guard moves to exit the room, Ranbir jumps from the table and tip toes behind the unsuspecting guard. Ranbir still has the guard's mobile in his hand. The guard has almost forgotten about it. Once; out in the corridor; without wasting time; Ranbir shoots the ground floor footage.

Exiting the laboratory, Ranbir finds himself in the corridor, ready to capture the much-needed footage of the ground floor.

Just opposite their experimentation room on the ground floor, there is a store room and adjacent to it is the staircase that leads to the second floor. Ranbir pushes the door of the store room open to find it full of boxes, mostly empty. The room has a large window that opens to the compound outside. He shoots its footage. Now is the time to send the footage to the commandoes.

Ranbir feeds Amruta's number, refreshes WhatsApp and hits the 'send' button. The uploading begins. But right in the middle of processing, the guard notices the baby, with his cell.

"How do you get out of that door every time?" the shocked guard exclaims, scooping up the baby in one hand and balancing a food plate in the other.

He takes him inside the laboratory.

"Give back my cell," the guard says as he keeps the child on the ground. Ranbir, in the meantime has already hit the back button and logged out of WhatsApp. Thankfully, the clip is sent. The job is done.

Amruta shows the clip to the Commando Chief. The Commando swiftly move to the planning table, ready to strategize with the vice commando and team to ensure a successful operation – an operation that would bring Mr. Kher and the baby back to safety and put an end to the reign of the dangerous Don.

"So, Mr. Kher, have you had your meal?" Dr. Denzongpa is in a spirited mood. "Here meet the Don himself." With a flourish, he presents the notorious Don.

The Don, who had kept himself hidden from the outside world to avoid any potential risks, now stood before Mr. Kher. So letting Mr. Kher see his face meant that Mr. Kher would surely be executed after the completion of the cloning project.

Expressing gratitude for Mr. Kher's cooperation, the Don's words were unexpectedly friendly. "Thanks for co-operating. I hope we achieve what we are about to embark upon. Just feel free to ask for whatever facilities you require", saying this, The Don offers a warm handshake. Mr. Kher reciprocates with a composed smile.

Soon, the D.N.A. samples from Don are taken and other requirements for the project are completed. The Don is escorted back to his room on the third floor. Dr. Denzongpa stays in the lab, overseeing the intricate procedures that are about to unfold.

After initiating the process of cloning, it would take 9 hours for the clone to come alive. Once alive the person would become a mortal man. This is the main concern of

Mr. Kher. As killing a mortal man after nine hours would amount to murder. Mr. Kher wants to badly communicate this to the boys but can't due to the constant presence of the guard and Dr. Denzongpa.

The large metallic cloning machine, stolen earlier from Mr. Kher's bungalow, is readied for action. The process is initiated. Mr. Kher's eyes fall on the led indicator, indicating the percentage of progress. The indicator says 'Initialising at 20.45 hours, which meant that the process would complete by 5.45 in the morning.

The hours tick away as the cloning process unfolds. Mr. Kher is handcuffed to chair again, his mind is consumed by the weight of his ethical dilemma. Somewhere around 1.45 a.m. Dr. Denzongpa leaves the room as there is nothing much to do other than wait till 5.45. a.m. He goes to rest in the guest room on the third floor adjoining the don's restroom. The laboratory guard is seen dozing at intervals. Mr. Kher takes the opportunity to speak out his concern to Ranbir. "The clone will start breathing by 5.45. a.m. We have to abort the process before that. Killing him after that would be like killing an innocent life. An act of murder."

"So what can we do about it?" Ranbir asks, concerned.

"We can only abort the process by damaging the machine. Just as we break an egg before the chicken hatches."

"It means... we have to destroy the machine and at the same time find a way to escape before 5.45 a.m, right?, Ranbir summarises, his mind racing to grasp the plan.

"And we even have to see that the guards are safe. We don't want to kill anybody"

"I will convey this to Sushant", saying this Ranbir slides down the table." Ranbir hurries beneath the table.

"Sushant, Mr. kher says that the machine needs to be destroyed before 5.45"

"Hey I think I can help. Ranbir you stay here, while I speak to Mr. Kher", says Sushant.

"What's the plan?", Ranbir gets excited.

"Have to speak with Mr. Kher first"

"O.K. Go up"

Sushant climbs upon the table.

"Mr. Kher, please check, if they have stock of TNT powder, ammonium chloride and HCl here"

Mr. Kher's eyebrows knit in confusion, but he quickly replies, "Yes, they do. Why do you ask?"

"We can blow up this place with those chemicals before the clone comes to life"

Mr. Kher's gaze sharpen as he processes the daring suggestion "Hmmm, the combination of these is lethal,"

"First, you have to be freed from the handcuffs," saying this Sushant crawls towards the guard who has dozed off. The handcuff keys are dangling from his pant pockets. Sushant's nimble fingers retrieve the keys from the guard's pocket, and with that, Mr. Kher is released form his restraints.

"This security guard would be killed in the blast. We can't let him die. Hope we can somehow send him out of this laboratory. This will help us make arrangements for the blast too", Mr. Kher voices his concerned.

"Idea!!! We can text the Commando Chief and instruct him to make a phone call on the guard's cell and call him out", Sushant exclaims.

"How would the commando have the guard's cellular number?" is a quick question by Mr. Kher.

Sushant's grin widens. "Remember the video clip sent by Ranbir on Amruta's cell. Amruta must have the number of sender'

"You are right. We can text Amruta and tell her to let the commandoes call on that number and call the guard out, brilliant idea!!!"

Sushant climbs down again.

"Let's try sending the text message informing Commandoes of the situation here," Sushant tells Ranbir

"O.k., What do you want to text?"

"Tell the Commandoes to call the security guard out, by calling on the number sent on Amruta's mobile, tell Commandoes we want to make arrangements for the blast, tell them to call the guard out exactly at 5.40 a.m."

"O.K.......done................Message sent!!!"

With the message on its way, the trio couldn't help but feel a renewed sense of hope, knowing that their allies are working tirelessly on the outside to assist their escape plan.

The Cloning work is in progress. The large cloning machine is doing its assigned task silently. The only indicator of the processing inside is the LED screen displaying the percentage of the process completed and the number of hours remaining.

Time ticks by. Now the indicator displays 10 minutes remaining'

Amruta conveys the message to the Commandoes. The Commandos are on high alert, ready to carry out the plan as instructed. It is a race against time, and every moment counted. Johnny is made to call on the guard's number.

"Who's this?", the sleeping guard is awakened. The guard is surprised as his was a very private number.

"How's my son?", Johnny asks from the other end

"Who are you and what son are you talking about?" says the surprised guard.

"The one who is with you at the moment."

"Who are you? How do you know that....Hello ...Hello", the guard is flummoxed.

"Hello ...hello ...your voice is breaking as you are in a closed room, come out," Johnny says

"*Ek minute,*" the guard goes out. Johnny keeps him engaged in his talks.

As soon as the guard leaves, Mr. Kher gets up and arranges the apparatus as per Sushant's instruction, "No sir, keep the flask here, on the right side of the test tube." Sushant directs Mr. Kher. He looks in full control. This time Sushant knows the difference between a flask and test tube. Ranbir climbs up and joins them.

"Sir get ammonium chloride immediately and put it in the flask. Take 67 mil of Hcl in the beaker. Dissolve it.", Sushant instructs. It is strange to see a commerce student giving instructions to someone of Mr. Kher's caliber.

"Ranbir fetch me that empty coke tin", Sushant points to a tin lying in a corner. "Tear open the top cover put TNT in it."

The timer on the cloning machine shows only two minutes left. Panic starts to set in as the situation becomes more critical. Rabbir quickly tears open the top of the coke tin.

"Quick... the clone will come alive", Ranbir panicks. Mr. Kher helps Ranbir to add the TNT powder contents to the tin.

"As soon as I say 'Now', Ranbir will kick and pour the contents of the tin in the flask" Sushant instructs Commando style.

"Yes, sir", Ranbir nods, ready for action.

"We'll position ourselves near the door so that we can escape quickly once Ranbir kicks the tin." Sushant says excitedly. "Sir, pick us both and run in the opposite store room after Ranbir Kicks"

Excitement and tension are in the air as the countdown continues, their plan hanging on a knife's edge. They know that their timing and execution has to be flawless to accomplish their mission.

The indicator displays '45seconds left'. Mr. Kher holds his nerves, his hands steady as he prepares to carry out his part of the plan. Sweat beads drop from Ranbir's forehead as he balances the tin on his right foot, his heart racing in anticipation.

"The time is now. Dost, everything depends on your skill now. Messi Zindabad!!!", Sushant embraces Ranbir. "*Bhai-Bhai*'. Ranbir braces himself.

The indicator says 5 seconds remaining.

"Now" orders Sushant.

Ranbir kicks the tin can containing TNT. The can flies It swirls in the air, spilling a little of its contents, mid-air. Mr. Kher picks up both the kids in his arms and pulls open the door. The can misses the flask and hits the wall behind it.

"Oh shit!!!", Sushant exclaims as he looks back from the arms of Mr. Kher.

The tin has hit the wall but the impact makes the chemical content in the tin can spill into the flask, mixing the chemicals. Just in the nick of time, Mr. Kher swings the door shut behind them.

BOOOOM!!! Flames jut from the room behind them.

The guard on the mobile gets alerted. Seeing Mr. Kher out of the room, he tries to get hold of him. But Mr. Kher skilfully enters the opposite store room and bolts the door from inside. A narrow escape.

Sushant checks his mobile. The mobile is dead. He tries to restart, but no luck. The trio are in jeopardy. The communication with the outside world is broken.

"In this room", the first guard shouts, pointing to the room to the two other guards. Soon the guards are against the door, yanking and kicking on it. Dr. Denzongpa joins them.

Mr. Kher holds against the door. He finds an iron cot, folded and kept against a wall. They put it against the door as a barrier. As they say a drowning man catches the straw.

"You are a dead man, Mr. Kher," rages Dr. Denzongpa. The smoke begins to spread in the air, a chilling reminder of the inferno they have triggered.

"Break the door," Dr. Denzongpa's order spur the guards into frenzied action. The pounding and kicking on the door increase, the iron cot rattling against the impact. Just in a matter of seconds, the door gives way. The iron cot is kicked aside by the guard and in comes Dr. Denzongpa, gun in hand.

Dr. Denzongpa, raging with anger, fire bullets haphazardly. Mr. Kher crouches on the opposite wall just below the window. Mr. Kher covers the babies but gets hit in back of the shoulder. Blood starts gushing out.

Just then, the window in the room breaks open. Splinters of glass fly in the air, and in comes the Commando chief. Firing the bullets while still in air, he makes a perfect landing on the floor.

The loyal guard valiantly attempts to shield Dr. Denzongpa, but the rain of bullets proves overwhelming. The guard crumples on the ground, lifeless. The other two guards get hit too.

Dr. Denzongpa dodges and tries to escape, but the continuous round from the Commandoes trigger ends his sinister journey. He falls backwards in the laboratory and is consumed by fire.

"As you sow so shall you reap," said Mr. Kher turning his gaze away from the ugly scene.

"Sir, you are bleeding. Are you O.K. Sir?" the Commando enquires.

"The portion of my shoulder is numb. I think it's the bullet inside," Mr. Kher says, feeling the blood.

Just then, more commandoes enter through the window and go out through the door in search of Don; their fire suit giving them protection from the fire. The heavy sound of rotating wings fills the space above the terrace. And then, like lightning descending from the heavens, the commandos descend on ropes from the hovering helicopter.

The terrace guards retaliate, but they are no match for the commandoes. The commandoes enter the farmhouse from all directions. The guards who surrender are handcuffed.

Terror surges through the don's veins as he watches commandoes come down from the terrace.

He picks up his gun and starts firing indiscriminately. His empire is now under siege, all his guards by now have been either killed or arrested.

In a desperate bid to defend himself, he runs back to his room. The commandoes kick on the closed door of his room, firing in between. The walls that had once shielded him are now closing in, suffocating his reign of terror.

The don panics and jumps out from the third floor. The ground rushes up to meet him, the impact jarring his bones. The gun he clutched so tightly is rendered useless. Pain sears through his body as he feels the fracturing of bones, his resilience shatters along with his empire.

The Commandoes have no trouble at all to set their hands on him. His dream of a free man was crushed forever.

The Chief Commando carries the babies and jumps out of the window onto the compound outside. Some Commandoes who are waiting outside offer help to Mr. Kher. Johnny and the girls who are standing at a distance during the whole operation, come running, smiles flood their nervous face.

"Are you all OK?", exclaims Amruta running towards them.

Ranbir's voice is urgent as he points to Mr. Kher "He's been hit in the shoulder, call the Ambulance fast"

"And what about you guys? Are you hurt?", Genelia asks.

"We are fine.", Sushant replies, a smile finally gracing his lips. Finally, he sees the caring expressions that he had longed to see.

Mr. Kher is made to sit inside a small country hotel a few yards away from the farmhouse. Mr. Kher sits on the bench, and the Chief Commando places the two children beside him. The Chief Commando gets a call from Vice Commando on his walkie-talkie.

"Sir, need orders to call an ambulance for the don, please come to the north end", the Vice Commando's voice crackled through the device.

"I will be there in a moment," the Chief commando responds before ending the call.

With a smile and a parting wink, he turns to the children, "I must say, you two deserve a bravery award," he praises before departing to attend to his duties.

"I would rather prefer the prize amount," Sushant says, looking at Genelia. Genelia's face falls at his words, a hint of disappointment clouding her expression.

Breaking the tension, Mr. Kher leans in, "You see Genelia, Sushant played a crucial role in orchestrating a blast using certain chemicals, and he's giving you the credit".

Genelia's surprise is palpable. "What? How?"

"Ammonium chloride, TNT and Hcl", he says with a triumphant grin.

Ammonium chloride was not necessary. Genelia says confused.

"Don't know, I just remember these thing from that day in the laboratory and your face."

"What!" Genelia blushes. Then suddenly taking a serious disposition she says, "If you had concentrated during your classes, you would have been a good student"

Sushant's grin only grows wider, "I would concentrate if I got teachers like you"

Everybody laughs.

THE PROMISE

A warm and lively atmosphere envelopes the hospital room as everyone gathers around Mr. Kher's bed. "How are you feeling now?" Johnny asks.

"I am fine and I think these guys don't mind staying in baby's body for a week more", smiles Mr. Kher, looking at the babies in their girlfriend's arms. The babies, along with the girls are staying at Johnny's house.

"Sir, take your time, sir, We are enjoying this," Sushant says, his hands around Genelia's neck,

"Sir, do get well soon and turn them back to what they were. We are dying to see them in their original Avatar," Amruta says.

"Sir, if you don't transform them back in a week, we will have to leave the babies with Johnny Uncle, alone, as we have our exams soon," Genelia says removing Sushant's hand from around her neck.

"What??? No way!" the babies say in unison along with Uncle Johnny.

Genelia continues with a smile, "Please warn them, no meeting for the next four months."

Amruta chimes in with a nod. "Exactly. Our college dean is like a hawk. If she catches us with boys, we'll be in big trouble."

"Yes, that would be done, right guys?", says Mr. Kher, looking at the saddened faces of babies. "They have to concentrate on their studies, right?"

Without looking up, the babies nodded a 'yes", a subtle pout of resignation on their faces.

The boys start a lingerie business in partnership. Surprisingly, their business does really well. Our Commerce guys have made it in the commercial world.

"It's been 3 full months, we haven't met them." Sushant says, his forehead on the counter.

"Chatting on WhatsApp just for half an hour every day is no fun" Ranbir complains.

"I want to be with her, badly", laments Sushant.

"Me too"

"But can't," says Mr. Kher, entering their shop. Both hung their head on the counter as though they were at the world's saddest party.

"Sir, do something. Want to be with them," Sushant says, raising his head.

"Can't stay without them, please sir" Ranbir raises his head too.

Mr. Kher looked at their pitiful faces; it's hard not to sympathise with them.

"O.k. I think I have a solution for you." Mr. Kher winks at them.

"What!!!!!!" the chaps are excited to know what Mr. Kher has in store for them.

It is the month of June, when the first rains touch the ground. Mother earth exudes the scent of the soil. The birds took hiding in the trees. Genelia and Amruta are in their jogging tracks returning from the gym, back to the hostel. Suddenly they hear sounds and ruffled moments in the bushes.

"Oh my, they will fall sick, Let's carry them to the hostel," says Amruta.

"Here's my towel," Genelia says.

The girls enter their hostel room.

"Quick, let's warm the water," Genelia says

As they go inside, the towel is pulled aside by two cute baby monkeys. Both the monkeys embrace each other '*Bhai Bhai...Bhai...Bhai*,' and wink with a naughty smile.

Boys will be Men!

www.ingramcontent.com/pod-product-compliance
Lightning Source LLC
LaVergne TN
LVHW090050160826
845672LV00015B/1622

* 9 7 9 8 8 9 7 2 4 1 0 7 1 *